USING THEORY TO EXPLORE HEALTH, MEDICINE AND SOCIETY

Peter Kennedy and Carole Ann Kennedy

This edition published in Great Britain in 2010 by

The Policy Press
University of Bristol
Fourth Floor
Beacon House
Queen's Road
Bristol BS8 1QU
UK

Tel +44 (0)117 331 4054
Fax +44 (0)117 331 4093
e-mail tpp-info@bristol.ac.uk
www.policypress.co.uk

North American office:
The Policy Press
c/o International Specialized Books Services (ISBS)
920 NE 58th Avenue, Suite 300
Portland, OR 97213-3786, USA
Tel +1 503 287 3093
Fax +1 503 280 8832
e-mail info@isbs.com

© The Policy Press 2010

British Library Cataloguing in Publication Data
A catalogue record for this book is available from the British Library.

Library of Congress Cataloging-in-Publication Data
A catalog record for this book has been requested.

ISBN 978 1 84742 401 3 paperback
ISBN 978 1 84742 402 0 hardcover

Cover design by Janna Broadfoot
Front cover: image kindly supplied by Paul Green
Printed and bound in Great Britain by Hobbs, Southampton

Contents

List of figures, tables and examples

Figures

Tables

Examples

To:

Mum and Dad,

Allen and Emma

Overview of the book

A major theme in the sociology of medicine literature is the extent to which society is coming under the influence of the expansion of medicine's jurisdiction into areas of personal and social relations, and the use of medical terminology to describe and explain more and more everyday interactions, behaviours and issues. Sociologists use the term 'medicalisation' to define this expansion. It is based on the idea that how we understand the social world – in this case through the medical gaze – has a large bearing on practice, because knowledge intervenes in the social world, helping to give it meaning and order, and ruling out what is and is not feasible. However, the sociology of medicine also plays an active/interventionist part, alongside medicine itself, in articulating practical orientations towards the medicalisation of society. Professionals recognise that their specialist body of knowledge has practical consequences. The profession of sociology is no different. Sociological knowledge has practical consequences in producing ideas about society and how it works and in shaping social practice. The sociology of medicine *produces ways of knowing* medicalisation: for example, some produce it as 'unassailable' or 'open to resistance' and therefore possibly reversible; some produce it as 'positive' and/or 'negative' in its outcomes; others as emanating solely from the institutions of medicine; and still others as a 'pervasive discourse' at large throughout society, largely adrift from the strict confines of medicine. Sociology also develops broader conceptual frames of reference, or grand narratives – for example, modernity, late modernity and so on – in producing knowledge of how we should know and act towards medicine and medicalisation.

Therefore, one of the major themes of this book is to assess the expanding influence of medicine into popular social issues such as obesity, binge drinking, happiness and therapy. At the same time another major theme of the book is to open up a discussion of how sociological theory and concepts play their part in *producing* or *representing* the dynamics of medicalisation. For example, conceptual frameworks that represent medicalisation in a negative light will have different causal implications for medical practitioners, social movements and policy makers, as will representations of medicalisation that stress its positive contributions. Similarly, the production of broader theoretical perspectives on society such as 'risk society', 'moral panic', 'late modernity', 'therapy culture' – all of which are discussed in the book – will also have practical consequences for how one approaches and takes action towards medicalisation. In this respect the book represents a sustained critical reflection on the impact that the above key theories and concepts have on our understanding and practical orientation towards the relationship between medicine, medicalisation and society.

Arguably, an approach reflexive of the combined causal influences of medicine and sociology is all the more necessary, given that over recent decades medicine and health have become highly political activities, rarely out of the public spotlight. Healthcare budgets, the authority of medicine, as well as our increasing preoccupation with daily health, are constant sources of media attention. Today we tend to be more sceptical of the proclamations of health experts, yet we also tend to be more engrossed with the daily minutiae of matters relating to our personal health and well-being. The risks associated with medicine and health interventions are debated publicly as never before, fuelled by the fact that we have never had so much health-related information at our disposal. Seemingly, the more information we have, the more scope there is for reinterpretation, and so the more that knowledge appears to be a source of conflict, debate and part of a struggle to contain, manage or distribute exposure to risk. Sociologists have long pointed out how medicine is extending its jurisdiction over ostensibly non-medical matters. This book is concerned with addressing what effects this has on the medicalisation thesis.

A recurring theme of the book is that a greater sense of public scrutiny and risk consciousness operates, in the wider movement within capitalism, between traditional modern society and high modernity. As umbrella terms for linking fundamental changes in work, leisure and families and the shifting boundaries between public and private domains, they are used in the book to help contextualise how broader social changes disrupt old certainties – creating opportunities for some and insecurities for many – and how this relates to the ongoing politicisation of health and medicine. Against this social backdrop the book examines the nature and authority of medicine and the challenges it faces under conditions of late-modern capitalism, with particular reference to how medicine's authority is both expanding and facing increasing scrutiny in the domains of self-help, obesity, binge drinking, anti-immunisation campaigns and alternative medicines, and what implications follow for an understanding of the medicalisation thesis. Key sociological themes and concepts will be used when and where appropriate to illuminate these key issues. Each chapter of the book concentrates on a popular health or medical topic and critically evaluates the explanatory power of different theories with respect to the topic under discussion.

Chapter One introduces some of the key figures in the sociology of medicine, who are drawn on to illuminate the book's underlying themes and examine, through the application of key sociological concepts, the dynamics of medicalisation in late-modern society. It is explained that while medicalisation may have its roots in the sick role (Parsons, 1951), be driven by social control aspirations (Zola, 1978) and be implicated in political power broking (Friedson, 1988), in all these activities it is fundamentally in a process of *social construction* that both medicine and the sociology of medicine are implicated. The implications of the latter are developed through a brief account of the medicalisation of mental illness. The chapter elaborates on the argument that not only medicine but also the sociology of medicine 'produce' medicalisation. In the sense that its main contributions to the area are *conceptual*, the sociology of medicine, it will be argued, is a means of producing knowledge about medicine's imperial ambitions as well as producing ways of articulating and knowing the meaning, extent and nature of medicalisation.

Chapter Two looks at the nature of modern medicine. The chapter examines the positive and negative outcomes of medical practice through the lens of critical political economy. The first section assesses the benefits and hazards of modern medicine, mostly in the UK. The chapter then attempts to understand the evidence furnished by drawing on two approaches to a critical political economy of medicine along the lines of the above definition. It describes and evaluates the work of Ivan Illich, who draws on a wider understanding of 'industrial society' to situate and understand the trajectory taken by modern medicine; and it then assesses the merits of Marxism, particularly the connections this perspective seeks to establish between developments in how medicine is organised and wider capitalist relations.

Chapter Three looks at the reasons behind the growing popularity of complementary and alternative medicine (CAM) in recent decades and what this implies for orthodox medicine. The chapter examines why complementary and alternative medicine has become so popular. In particular, it considers to what extent the growing popularity of CAM has been driven by a pervasive disenchantment with the public's experiences of orthodox medicine or simply by an irrational attack on scientific knowledge. It discusses how and why this disenchantment may be facilitated and underpinned by broader social transformations, including what Giddens describes as the shift from traditional modern society to late (or high) modernity. Finally, the chapter draws on Habermas's concepts of 'systems world' and 'life world' to help assess the extent to which CAM resists the forces of instrumental rationality and the imperatives of the systems world.

Chapter Four reflects on another apparent dilemma facing medical science: we seek the assistance and authority of medical science, while at the same time we appear to question the validity of its claims and worry over the objectivity of its findings, sometimes to the point where we are unsure about what to believe in areas affecting our health and well-being. To assess this dilemma the chapter discusses the example of the MMR (measles, mumps and rubella) controversy and why it strikes a chord with the core characteristics of what Beck defines as 'risk society'. The chapter then goes on to examine the merits of the concept of risk society for a broader understanding of the contradictory location of medical science in modern society. The chapter assesses whether the concept of risk society provides useful insights into the dilemmas facing medical science, noting that risk consciousness is not homogenous, but highly variable according to social context and place.

Chapter Five addresses the issue of therapy and happiness. The chapter presents a critique of the happiness literature and considers how the search for happiness is closely associated with the prevalence of personal counselling services throughout society and the burgeoning interest in therapies like cognitive behaviour, client-centred therapy, goal-directed therapy; relationship therapies; emotional therapy; anger management counselling; and therapies to enhance 'emotional intelligence'. The chapter then relates the happiness and therapy industry to broader social changes associated with high modernity and evaluates the view that the 'happiness industry' is part of a much wider cultural shift in which relationships become increasingly mediated in terms of the personal, the psychological and the emotive and less in terms of the collective bonds between people.

Chapter Six looks at the present concern with obesity. Obesity is portrayed as an unstoppable epidemic, out of control and threatening to reverse the achievement of increased longevity in the developed world. How accurate are these claims? The chapter outlines the official definition of obesity and describes recent statistical trends that emerge from this definition, before identifying three paradigms for understanding obesity: *medical, social structural* and *social construction*. The chapter goes on to discuss how the medical paradigm offers key insights into obesity but fails to take account of the social structural factors central to the rise in obesity. On the other hand, accounts that posit social structural causes of obesity tend to objectify obesity as a fact and so tend to ignore or play down how obesity is socially constructed by a range of social factors, including both the medical and social discourses. The chapter concludes by arguing that all three paradigms – *medical, social structural* and *social construction* – are crucial to an understanding of why obesity is a key issue in contemporary society.

Chapter Seven examines the theme of moral panics related to binge drinking. Over the last decade news media coverage portraying negative images of anti-social, binge-drinking youth has quickened in pace. The tabloid press has led the way with lurid stories about escalating incidents of binge drinking, which is now seen as the new 'British disease'. The UK government and the British Medical Association too have expressed their growing concern with an epidemic of binge drinking, among youth in particular. The chapter examines the concept of moral panic as a way of approaching binge drinking from a different angle; one that does not assume that it is an object outside of social meaning. Here emphasis shifts to examining for whom drinking is a social problem, which social groups are defining binge drinking and which interests are served by such definitions. The chapter concludes that if we embed the concept of 'binge drinking' in wider social structural changes affecting youth today, we can better articulate why the nature of binge drinking is both an objective reality *and* an object of social construction related to sustaining the existing social order.

In summary, the book draws together within one volume debates surrounding a range of popular issues in health, medicine and society. It is written for those who are unconvinced that social theory can be of practical use to everyday issues in health, medicine and society, and those who are wary of the difficulties and complexities of theory. Increasingly, social theory has to explain and justify its existence, not only to non-social science students, but also to students whose studies are centrally concerned with social theory, and so with issues of power, social control, social conflict and social inequality. Social theory is sometimes judged to be little more than an academic luxury, challenged by the belief that it is better to get on with the real task of collecting evidence about what is going on and looking at the diverse opinions about what implications follow. The mantra 'why do we need social theory anyway?' emerges as the logical correlate. We can certainly gain a lot from empirically studying areas such as binge drinking, the development of self-help, debates about MMR, and so on, by noting, for example, which groups are involved, what definitions there are about the object of our enquiry and recording the rate at which the social issue, problem or phenomenon occurs in any given population. Without the latter, theory is useless abstraction. Yet without theory, empirical findings lack coherence and meaning.

At the heart of the book is the belief that social theory always plays its part in producing the social world it seeks to explain and change, but that it remains crucial to illuminating social issues in socially progressive ways: it is not whether one should use social theory or not, but how to use social theory in a practical way to illuminate how popular issues in health and medicine harbour social power disparities and can illuminate broader social changes occurring today.

References

Friedson, E. (1988) *Profession of medicine: A study of the sociology of applied knowledge*, Chicago, IL: Chicago University Press.

Parsons, T. 1964 (1951) *The social system*, New York: The Free Press.

Zola, I. (1978) 'Medicine as an institution of social control' in J. Ehrenreich (ed), *The cultural crisis in modern medicine*, New York: Monthly Review Press, pp 80-100.

ONE

Introduction: medicine, medicalisation and society

In the overview of this book it was observed how, in recent decades, medicine and health have become highly political activities rarely out of the public spotlight. Healthcare budgets, the authority of medicine, as well as our increasing preoccupation with daily health, are a constant source of media attention. As a population we are more sceptical of the proclamations of health experts, yet more engrossed with the daily minutiae of matters of personal health and well-being. The risks associated with medicine and health interventions are debated as never before, even though we have never had so much health-related information at our disposal. The more information we have, the more scope there is for reinterpretation of medical pronunciations, so the more knowledge appears to be a source of conflict, debate and part of a struggle to contain, manage or distribute exposure to health risks.

Despite this, the medical model continues to enjoy high status in society. People may contest it and have alternative social models to draw upon in doing so. Nevertheless, the medical model remains a dominant paradigm in the West, so much so that governments will rarely admit to making healthcare and medicine bear the brunt of budget cuts. Its continued dominance is partly due to the medical model's strong links with science. Drawing upon scientific explanations, medicine operates with a biological/infectious disease model of illness (Senior and Viveash, 1998, pp 10–12). The main site of the 'disease' is the individual and their biological functioning. Adhering to 'germ theory' as the *sine qua non* of disease, illness is located in physical, biological and genetic abnormalities within the body (White, 2002, pp 36–7). The scientific worldview to which medicine ascribes is one in which observable reality (facts) are assumed to exist outside of the scientist, doctor or psychiatrist, who can, with the aid of the scientific method, observe these 'facts' without too much prejudice creeping in to distort findings and analysis (Smith, 1998). Moreover, the object of scientific inquiry (be it physical, biological or mental 'matter') is said to exhibit clearly observable patterns or behaviours, from which regularities can be detected and causal inferences can be made about the nature of the object and what is normal or abnormal to its development (Smith, 1998). The point is that these assumptions about how science operates are, for the most part, held in great esteem by society. Although under serious challenge in some quarters of society, the common-sense view is that science can achieve mostly what it claims to achieve in terms of being (relatively) value free and able to gain access to facts and causes so as to progress knowledge of the physical and social world and make positive interventions. Furthermore, because medicine is thought to be a *key application of science to the human body* it is able to bask in the afterglow of the latter's continuing, if increasingly scrutinised, social reputation (Senior and Viveash, 1998). Hence the medical model remains paradigmatic even though it is placed under increasing scrutiny and contested because people still expect it to be right and hold the answers to health issues, from cures, to the expansion of medical advice, to the management of further areas of social life deemed to be a source of health-related risks. This continued paradigmatic status is given expression by the term 'medicalisation', which has become a bedrock concept in sociological literature in the area of medicine, health and society.

Medicalisation

Medicalisation refers to the expansion of medical jurisdiction into areas traditionally thought to be non-medical (Szasz, 2007, p 1). As a fixed reference point, the definition is simple and accurate; however, the reality is that as a *process* it is frustratingly difficult to pin down with such accuracy. Medicalisation is complicated because the lines between medical and non-medical domains are often blurred and fluid rather than neatly separated; where they lie with respect to obesity, binge drinking and alternative therapies, for example, cannot so easily be ascertained. The relationship between each domain is the outcome of the complex articulation of medical science, competing professional objectives, patient interest groups and wider political interests. However, despite the complexities involved, sociologists have sought to disentangle some of the main interlinking factors in the medicalisation process with respect to what appear to be ostensibly non-medical domains.

For Parsons (1964), medicine is the science of classifying, treating and curing disease; and the medical profession, which bases itself on expert knowledge, has the legitimate authority to make any necessary judgements about what divides medical from non-medical domains. However, Parsons also highlights the social domains of medicine, and with them, a basis for medicalisation, in the 'doctor-patient relationship'. Medicine, therefore, has a dual domain: it discloses and eradicates disease and negotiates 'disease' into 'sickness'. The two are not always identical. While you or I may have a medically defined disease, we may not be sick. Sickness, as Parsons observes, is a 'social fact' that emerges from the negotiations between doctor and patient corresponding to their wider social roles. One may have a disease but not be officially 'sick'. Alternatively, one may feel sick or claim to be so, but not have a disease. On the one hand, the individual must adopt the role of 'patient' in order to access the 'sick role'. The sick role makes it socially legitimate for them to take leave from their normal social responsibilities, including those involved with work and the family. On the other hand, the individual is called upon to play their role by taking medical advice and treatment to get well. For Parsons, then, the ground for establishing what is medical and non-medical as well as the grounds for medicalisation are the outcome of the functional relationship between legitimate medical practice to diagnose and 'cure' disease and the function performed by the sick role in sanctioning individuals who deviate from social norms and responsibilities.

Parsons highlights the social function of medicine in suggesting the driving force of medicalisation. Zola (1978, p 254), on the other hand, highlights the *social control* aspirations of medicine as the main driving force in medicalising society, 'nudging aside religion and law' as the repository of truth by redefining virtue and legitimacy in terms of health with respect to the 'good practices of life'. Zola identifies four themes driving medicine's expanding social control function. Firstly, medicine has broadened out its initial focus on biology to incorporate social and psychological factors influencing disease and illness, such as psychosomatic and wider environmental influences. Secondly, medicine is able to use the legitimate control it has won over the right to carry out surgical procedures, prescribe drugs and so on, and apply them to an expanding assortment of 'diseases', from plastic surgery, safe sex, the extension of life through heart, liver or kidney transplantations, to 'hyperactive' children and a variety of stress-related 'syndromes', and so on. Thirdly, Zola argues that medicine expands its jurisdiction into areas of life once deemed social or natural but which increasingly fall under biomedically defined norms of health, for example, medicine's expansion into the life cycle from cradle to grave: pregnancy/childbirth, child development, getting older, and so on. Fourthly, medical advice has expanded into all aspects of what constitutes 'the good life', where the emphasis is not so much on illness but on healthier individuals too; for example, through the expanding domains of health promotion into the benefits of exercise, diet, work–life balance strategies, and so on (Zola, 1978).

Friedson (1988, p 23) moves more explicitly towards the political aspects of medicine, to identify the dual role of political and medical institutions as organisational forces in society driving forward the medicalisation process. As Friedson observes, the 'foundation of medicine's control over its work is … political in character, involving the aid of the state in establishing and maintaining the profession's pre-eminence'. In this respect, medicine's power to set itself apart from rivals (whether they be alternative medicines or related health and social care professions) is, for Friedson, based on the capacity to forge itself into an identifiable occupational group, separated from others by the germ theory of illness and disease and sharing a similar background of training in medical schools. Developing this scientific and organisational prowess helped medicine to gain recognition from the state as the 'arbiter of medical work'. The state gained from this relationship because, as Illich (1976) observed, modern medicine was industrial in scope, offering quick medical fixes on a mass scale resembling mass production techniques forming the basis of industrial society and founded on narrow definitions of illness and health which assisted in the wider political and social task of dividing populations into neat classifications of productive/unproductive, disabled/able bodies. Moreover, medicine could be drawn upon by the state to depoliticise decisions made about the distribution of public resources aimed at various forms of welfare (Friedson, 1988). For example, where medicine is free at the point of need, as is still by and large the case today in the UK and the National Health Service (NHS), then medicine can be invoked to separate 'medical' (free) from 'social' (means-tested) care and, therefore, set limits to the costs incurred by the state for 'free care'.

In summary, medicalisation has its roots in the sick role, is driven by social control aspirations and is implicated in political power broking. Yet in all these activities it is fundamentally a process of *social construction* (Friedson, 1988). The concept of social construction points to the merging of facts into values and the idea that social objects and the facts one observes about such objects are what interacting social subjects collectively define them to be. In this respect, Parsons' designation of the 'sick role', Zola's four driving themes of medicalisation and Friedman's power broking within government over health and social care are examples of how medicine's domains of influence in society are acts of social construction. For Berger and Luckmann (1991 [1967]), the social construction of reality refers to the way in which people interact with each other and enter sometimes reciprocal, sometimes conflicting, roles through which they create, foster and share contested meanings and concepts which they act upon and which form the basis of their social practice, to the point where those meanings and actions become inscribed in institutions and embedded in society as 'objective truths' or simply taken-for-granted assumptions.

Social constructionist perspectives differ over the extent to which they allow a social reality outside of what is produced by the shared meanings and activities of people, with one end of the spectrum rejecting a separate reality and downplaying human agency and the other end subscribing to some belief in a reality beyond the social construction of reality, but with the relative independence of social agents intact (Burr, 1995). Nevertheless, all social constructionists seek to challenge the very idea of there being objective truths about the body and illness to which medical science claims to have direct access. If we take obesity, for example, Turner (2008, p 149) suggests that 'obesity is not an empirical characteristic of unregulated bodies, but the effect of a language about bodies'. The body per se, as well as issues emerging from the body, such as weight and shape, provides a powerful means of governing what is normal as opposed to abnormal within populations (Turner, 2008).

This claim about the body as a signifier of social relations can be more practically understood by reflecting for a moment on how we relate to and make sense of each other through a multitude of body-related symbols. We buy brand-named clothes and foods, sometimes because we think the quality is better than non-branded, but for the most part because we are buying into a system of meanings about how we wish to be perceived by others in the social pecking order. In this respect, branded goods are purchased not only for their intrinsic value but also for what they symbolise for us and what we think they symbolise for others (Allen et al, 2007). Indeed, our dress sense, manner of expression, the roles we play out as mother, father, sister, brother, worker, manager, professional, and so on, are all symbols through which we relate to others. There is nothing reducibly natural or intrinsic about any of these symbols; they are social constructions which give off social information about us and our place in the social world. Of course, roles change and we challenge and often resist ascribed social roles as much as we embrace them, but nevertheless, they are inherent to social order and indeed to social control. As Douglas notes,

> The social body constrains the way the physical body is perceived. The physical experience of the body ... sustains a particular view of society. There is a continual exchange of meaning between the two kinds of bodily experience so that each reinforces the other. (Douglas, 1970, p 93)

The implication here is that control over the body is a principal means of effecting social control over people both individually and collectively. We see the intermeshing of body and symbolic meaning most clearly in everyday sayings in which the natural body becomes a vehicle to express moral sentiments: 'have a heart', 'cold-blooded', 'thick-skinned', 'gutless', 'chinless', 'spineless', 'under-hand'. Body parts are also social metaphors for moral statements about how people act or how they ought to act. As Turner (see above) might say in the case of obesity and weight generally, 'so it is with body shape'. The shape and the weight of our body are also metaphors for moral statements about how we ought to live our lives according to the social norms and morals of our society. The current focus on body size and the special attention to being 'too thin' or 'overweight' symbolises something about society and how normal body shape is defined and regulated as much as it pronounces on the health of an individual. The concern with obesity perhaps informs us more about the social preoccupation with the ideal body. It symbolises a society in which the pressure to 'keep up appearances' is immense. Individuals are exhorted to eat out but eat healthily, exercise regularly but preferably through membership of a private gym and, if we do succumb to bodily temptation, then we must expect to do our penance in the form of dieting – with the aid of the diet industry of course.

If social construction is the key characteristic of medicalisation as a social *process*, then two of the key *mechanisms* in this 'construction' process (intimated in the above examples) are those of *labelling* and *discourse*. Both of the latter play crucial productive parts as conceptual frameworks for understanding the nature and significance given to processes of medicalisation. Indeed, not only medicine but also the sociology of medicine 'produces' medicalisation. The sociology of medicine has its own means of production: it is both a means of producing knowledge(s) about medicine's imperial ambitions and a means of producing ways of articulating and knowing the meaning, extent and nature of medicalisation. We can observe this dual productive role in the following two extended examples of labelling and discourse in the medicalisation of mental illness, set out in **Examples 1.1** and **1.2**.

Example 1.1: Labelling and medicalisation, with reference to mental illness

Becker (1963) applied the concept of labelling to an understanding of how social order is negotiated and constructed. Labelling operates in two directions: in the direction of the reaction of the social group to the behaviour of the individual, and in how the individual (deviant) reacts to the social group. If the reaction is one way, the label may not be internalised by the individual, who may then reject outright or be resistant to the way they are being labelled. Becker defined labelling as the process whereby socially defined identities are imposed or adopted, leading to the stigmatisation of an individual or group. Here stigmatisation refers to the process in which forms of social behaviour become the subject of social disapproval, resulting in a spoiled identity (Hebl and Kleck, 2002, p 128).

Manning (2001) argues that psychiatry responds to three specific pressures: professional, social/legal and technical. *Professionally*, psychiatry is dependent for its high social status on maintaining its scientific links with biomedicine and the disease model. *Socially*, psychiatry's professional autonomy is dependent on the legal entitlement to practise that is given to it by the state. Psychiatry is therefore susceptible to pressure from the state and society to explain deviancy that calls into question what is 'normal' as opposed to 'abnormal' behaviour – and so what may be threatening to social order in the more definitive and apparently neutral terms of reference assigned to science and biomedicine. *Technically*, psychiatry, faced with having to deal with mental health user groups and other professions related to mental disorder, such as social work, is compelled to draw some closure over knowledge by imposing a classification system that fixes individuals as 'mentally ill'. It does this in such a way as to claim certainty of diagnosis when in reality there is only complexity and ambiguity. In other words, while not forgetting the scope for resistance, psychiatry is under pressure to label individual behaviours as 'signs' of mental disorder; 'signs' that, we need to remind ourselves, have no direct causal basis in biology.

Psychiatry claims the ability to cluster sets of observed behaviours and signs of disease into *classifications* (labels) *of mental illness*, as laid out in the two dominant systems of classification, the American-based 4th edition of the *Diagnostic and Statistical Manual*, DSM-iv (American Psychiatric Association, 2000) and the World Health Organization's 10th edition of *International Classification of Disease*, ICD-10 (WHO, 1994). That there are fourth and tenth editions implies that classifications have undergone considerable changes over the years, which since the 1940s has led to the need to modify or remove some classifications and invent others. For example, in the first editions homosexuality was classified as a mental illness, as was alcoholism. And in the later editions there has been a greater concern to construct classifications of 'personality disorder'. In general, psychiatry claims to have discovered three broad classifications of mental illness along the lines of neurosis, psychosis and personality disorder. It has also broken each of these broader classifications down into finer classifications, for example, 'neurosis' covers types of depression and anxiety syndromes, and 'psychosis' covers classifications such as schizophrenia. The socially constructed nature of these labels or classifications can be seen simply by comparing the two manuals on any given classification.

ICD-10 and DSM-iv differentiate between several 'personality disorders', as is shown by the classification in **Table 1.1**.

Table 1.1: ICD-10 and DSM-iv classifications of 'personality disorder'

Description	ICD-10	DSM-iv
Shows great social detachment and is restricted in emotional expressions and is indifferent to emotional expressions of others and not interested in social relationships.	Schizoid PD	Schizoid PD
Social and interpersonal deficits marked by acute discomfort with, and reduced capacity for, close relationships.		Schizotypal PD
Characterised by instability, impulsivity, recklessness, explosiveness.	Emotionally unstable PD Explosive type Borderline type Aggressive type	Borderline PD
Too strong self-importance. Exaggerates own capabilities and achievements.	Other specific PDs, eccentric, 'unstable' type, narcissistic passive-aggressive	Narcissistic PD

As we can see, the ICD-10 and DSM-iv systems vary in the way they classify (label) personality disorder. (For example, 'Social and interpersonal deficits marked by acute discomfort with, and reduced capacity for, close relationships' come under quite different signs – schizoid and schizotypal – while the description 'Too strong self-importance. Exaggerates own capabilities and achievements' is linked to multiple signs in ICD-10 and only one in DSM-iv.) Yet, despite the differences, they both concur that personality disorder is objective and factually observable enough to be amenable to classification in the first place. However, it is more reasonable to assume that because neither science nor medicine has established any link between a person's biology and 'their' mental health, then the classifications are held to 'stand in' for the underlying (and as yet unknown, but presumed knowable) biological or chemical cause. Therefore, individuals who are observed to have the tell-tale number of interlinking behaviours and signs are classified as 'having' a mental illness or 'being' mentally ill and exhibiting specific 'diseases', such as schizophrenia, for example.

The above example of the socially constructed nature of mental illness classifications through the process of labelling demonstrates in stark fashion the role of medicine (here the branch of psychiatry) in medicalising behaviours associated with mental health. However, sociology has also played a role in producing an understanding of mental illness as an act of labelling. The productive role of sociology perhaps becomes clearer once we reflect on other sociological takes on the social construction of mental illness. But before we proceed, an example of the discourse approach to social construction is instructive.

Example 1.2: Discourse and medicalisation, with reference to mental illness

Discourse refers to ways of knowing and acting in society through language, texts and practices. To state that discourse and discourses construct society is to claim that how we act in the world is shaped by how we know the social world. Dominant forms of knowledge relating to the medical model, for example, shape our understanding of what constitutes health and illness and the boundaries between the latter and non-medical matters. Seen as a discourse, the medical model is a way of knowing the body and how it functions. This discourse is promoted in practice by the development of specialist groups who define the area of knowledge and internalise the discourse. In turn, the lay public internalise this discourse and take on the role of 'patient' by subscribing, more often implicitly, to the knowledge and practices associated with the medical model.

Discourses are not visible, but are deep, underlying structures that give social meaning and order to the way we live our lives. They define intimate relationships between social meaning, social practices and our understanding of the latter. Discourses, like labelling, are a source of social control and discipline over individuals. They are forms of moral regulation of what is permissible and what is normal/abnormal. The crucial thing to bear in mind is that discourses change over time, not in a discrete and linear fashion, but in the form of overlapping tendencies which influence and over-determine each other. Discourse alerts us to how labels, for example of madness, are never fixed but are open to change and transformation. Discourse differs from labelling theory because it emphasises structures of meaning that create subjects and their objects, and not predefined agents, intersubjectively creating the social world. Michel Foucault (1976) understood mental illness as a discourse: a system of meanings, practices and knowledge that marks out the grounds of mental health and illness. As Huxley observes, 'Foucault wishes to disassociate the idea of the subject from humanist philosophies that postulate transcendental human will and intention as the source of historical change and social relations' (Huxley, 2008, p 1636). Foucault (1976) pointed out how the discourse of madness as a signifier of witchcraft came prior to, and then overlapped in time with, the belief that madness is an illness located in the brain, and how the latter then overlapped with the belief that madness is a socially constructed stigma ascribed to those who flout social norms or are perceived as socially undesirable or dangerous.

Prior to the 18th century the discourse of mental disorder had not yet become dominant in how madness was known and understood. One could be mad, and madness was certainly well known, but one could not be mentally ill, simply because society did not think/practise in such terms. The role of medicine and proto psychiatry within the first asylums that arose in Europe in the 18th century was to manage the mad through forms of therapy and moral tutorship. According to Foucault (1976), until around the end of the 18th century, asylums for the 'mad' were sites of moral therapy and social control. At this point in history, medicine and psychiatry, although largely ineffectual as a form of treatment, had become dominant over who was to be admitted, what treatment should be meted out and for how long. But as yet medicine and the fledgling psychiatric discipline had not defined madness in terms of biomedicine, and so, of mental illness. The decision to incarcerate in this period was driven by legal/bureaucratic/moral rules and not by biomedicine. However, this situation was soon to change, because by the late 18th and early 19th centuries the medical profession began to take control over the regulation of asylums. Medicine had gradually come under the influence of positivist science (Romano, 2002). As outlined at the beginning of this chapter, science claimed that the study of the body and society should be conducted in the same way as one would study the natural object, and its views began to hold sway in elite medical circles, which is the hallmark of positivism. Specifically, the belief that the tools of natural science – observation, hypothesis, testing/experimentation, deducing of laws and so on – were the ideal tools with which to approach illness of the body and mind in order to effect a cure began to hold sway within medicine.

The influence of positivist science, as a basis for medical theory and practice, on the redefinition of madness as mental illness was crucial. However, the latter was also supported by what Foucault refers to as the 'urge to classify'. For although the urge to classify scientifically has a history stretching back to the classical age, for Foucault this classification was limited, by the existing level of knowledge, to descriptions of madness based on unreason, supernatural, and so on. Moreover, classification was also limited to the existing level of botanic taxonomy based on humeral treatments. In fact it was not until Darwin's extensive work on classification in the mid/late 19th century and the development of germ theory, and so on, that such taxonomies began to inform overall theories of life in general: before that, taxonomies provided no conception of what made life possible within the body.

Thus, the development to dominance of psychiatry was based on a shift in discourses about madness; madness came under the sign of 'mental disorder' and this shift, in turn, depended on psychiatry's links with medicine and positivist science, in conjunction with the developing classification system of illnesses. As Foucault (2001, p xii) put it:

> In the serene world of mental illness, modern man no longer communicates with the madman; on the one hand, the man of reason delegates the physician to madness, ... on the other hand, the man of madness communicates with society only by the intermediary of an equally abstract reason which is to order physical and moral constraint, the anonymous pressure of the group, the requirements of conformity.

These brief examples help one to understand that labelling and discourse as an activity engaged in by sociologists (their means of production, so to speak) 'produce' *different* accounts of medicalisation for consumption by the reader. Let us consider this more closely. On the one hand, labelling is a theoretical tool produced by sociology to assist in illuminating the role played by interacting social agents in the negotiation and classification of behaviours and identities related to mental illness. Emphasis is placed on active social agents in negotiation with each other in the construction of mental illness categories. On the other hand, discourse as a theoretical tool has no such central role for agents, but instead ascribes centrality to the structures of shared language, texts and practices; individuals come into the gaze through the latter and their actions are understood in terms of the structures, rather than the other way around as with labelling, which places emphasis on a negotiated order between active social agents. Discourse points to how agents become subjects within the medical model, where networks of meaning, language and texts provide social agents with a worldview guiding their actions and marginalising other ways of knowing (for example, complementary and alternative models of medicine). Discourse also sheds light on competing models. We saw, with Foucault, how discourses of madness (what it is to know 'madness' and to 'be mad') shift over time; at one time madness becomes knowable to us (becomes socially constructed) through reference to supernatural forces; at other times, prior to industrial capitalism and the ascendancy of scientific classification systems, the discourse of madness is much more of a social model (to be mad is to be interwoven with other 'anti-social' people such as vagrants or beggars or with 'non-productive' members of society, such as people with disabilities, orphans or elderly people). With the advent of industrial capitalism and the rise to dominance of modern science, medicine became central to developing the medical model or discourse of mental illness, to which we referred above.

The central point here is that while social construction is central to knowing the role played by medicine in the medicalisation of society, we come to know social construction in subtly different ways, through competing sociological frames of reference. In other words, the sociology of medicine is itself engaged in *different social constructions* of medicalisation. We could liken this to gazing through different windows looking out onto the same process from different angles; if each social construction is a window, then each window provides us with a different vantage point on medicalisation. Only, rather than competing in a zero-sum game of 'true' versus 'false' knowledge, each window adds to the stock of knowledge about medicalisation. For example, labelling is one way of constructing medicalisation, discourse provides another, while both add to our sum of knowledge concerning the dynamics of medicalisation. Moreover, these different gazes or mechanisms of 'knowing medicalisation' – labelling and discourse – have a causal aspect to them: for, as we saw in the brief overview of mental illness, they serve to create how we come to 'know medicalisation'.

In this very important sense, the sociology of medicine 'produces' medicalisation, no less than medicine and the state, and, indeed, Parsons' 'sick role', do. Professional sociologists produce medicalisation in the sense that they construct *conceptual contexts* or frames of reference through which medicine's expanding domain in society is given meaning and shape. For example, a sociology of medicine from a Marxist perspective will produce a very different conceptual context for understanding the meaning and importance to society of medicalisation processes than, for example, Illich did; or if one applied Habermas's conceptual framework of 'system' and 'life world' dynamics within the wider conceptual context of 'late modernity', then a different production of medicalisation would emerge, and so on. This is not to say that one perspective and conceptual framework holds the secret and others miss the point, rather it is to recognise (1) that the defining contribution which the sociology of medicine has made and continues to make to the study of the relationship between medicine and society is dependent on the conceptual tools it brings to bear; (2) that the different conceptual tools may differ, but they nevertheless add to our stock of knowledge about the interface between medicine and society; and (3) that this stock of knowledge is a productive act which has causal significance for an understanding of, in this case, the extent (or otherwise) and nature of medicalisation and how we practically relate to this process.

As we observed at the beginning of this chapter, Parsons, Zola, Friedson and Conrad (1992) have developed profound insights into the social and political imperatives driving the medicalisation of society, and much has been written since on the roles of both labelling and discourse as powerful mechanisms underpinning the socially constructed nature of medicalisation. The aim of this book is to highlight the ways in which popular issues such as obesity, binge drinking, therapy and happiness are increasingly falling within the medical domain. Another aim is to highlight the productive role that key sociological concepts have in relation to the meaning and significance given to medicalisation. Each of the chapters to follow will focus on one or two key sociological concepts in relation to a specific area bearing on the relationship between health, medicine and society. In each case the aim is twofold: to highlight the contribution of sociology to an understanding of the shifting and uncertain interfaces between health, medicine and society that provide pathways and resistances to medicalisation; and to recognise that sociological knowledge is itself a productive act in constructing the way we know and come to understand the latter.

The content of this book

We noted earlier that while Parsons (1964) highlights the social function of medicine as the driving force of medicalisation, for Zola (1978, p 254), the social control aspirations of medicine are the main driving force in medicalising society, 'nudging aside religion and law' as the repository of truth by redefining virtue and legitimacy in terms of health with respect to the 'good practices of life'.

Chapter Two takes up Zola's claim through a detailed account of the work of Illich and of the Marxist approach to the political economy of the impact of modern medicine and its implications for medicalisation. In particular, Chapter Two situates medicine in modern capitalist industrial society and its commodity structure, as a context for understanding modern medicine and the dynamics of medicalisation. The chapter examines the positive and negative outcomes of medicalisation through the lens of critical political economy. The first section assesses the benefits and hazards of modern medicine, mostly in the UK. The chapter then attempts to understand the evidence furnished by drawing on two approaches to a critical political economy of medicine. We will describe and evaluate the work of Ivan Illich, who draws on a wider understanding of 'industrial society' to situate and understand the trajectory taken by modern medicine and the medicalisation process, before assessing the merits of Marxism, particularly the connections it seeks to establish between the benefits and costs of medicalisation, against the conceptual backdrop of developments in how medicine is organised within wider capitalist relations and the commodity structure of the economy.

It was also noted earlier that medicine and health have become highly political activities of late, rarely out of the public spotlight. Healthcare budgets, the authority of medicine, as well as our increasing preoccupation with daily health, are a constant source of media attention. As a population we are more sceptical of the proclamations of health experts, yet more engrossed with the daily minutiae of matters of personal health and well-being. To come to some understanding of why this is so and what significance it has for the interface between health, medicine and society, Chapter Three compares and contrasts the very different approaches to the concept of 'late modernity' (or 'high modernity'), offered by Giddens and Habermas as the intellectual prism through which to evaluate and examine the reasons for the growing popularity of complementary and alternative medicine (CAM) in recent decades and then come to terms with what this implies for medicine and the dialectic between processes of *medicalisation* and *demedicalisation*. In particular, the chapter considers to what extent the growing popularity of CAM has been driven by a pervasive disenchantment with the public experience of orthodox medicine. It also considers how and why this disenchantment may be facilitated and underpinned by broader social transformations, including what Giddens describes as the shift from traditional modern society to late modernity; and to what extent Habermas's concepts of 'systems world' and 'life world' can help to provide a theoretical framework for a more nuanced understanding of the relationship between CAM and orthodox medicine as part rapprochement and part repulsion.

The risks associated with medicine and health interventions are debated as never before, even though we have never had so much health-related information at our disposal. The more information we have, the more scope there is for reinterpretation of medical pronunciations, and so the more knowledge appears to be a source of conflict, debate and part of a struggle to contain, manage or distribute exposure to health risks. Chapter Four examines the concept of 'risk society' (Beck, 1992) as a means of making sense of an apparent contradiction, which is that we increasingly seek the assistance and authority of medical science, while at the same time we appear to question the validity of its claims and worry over the objectivity of its findings, to the point where we are unsure about what to believe for the best in areas affecting our health and well-being. To what extent does the latter act as a means to resist medicalisation, or to what extent does it provide fertile ground? To assess this dilemma and what it signifies for medicalisation, the chapter discusses the example of the MMR controversy and why it strikes a chord with the core characteristics of what is a 'risk society'. The chapter argues that the concept of risk society provides useful insights into the dilemmas facing medical science, yet also notes that risk consciousness is not homogenous, but is highly variable according to social context and place.

Chapter Five draws on the concept of *therapy culture* (Furedi, 2004) to consider the public preoccupation with defining and achieving happiness, and the development of a counselling industry in recent decades. The chapter considers how the search for happiness is closely associated with the prevalence of personal counselling services throughout society and the burgeoning interest in therapies such as cognitive behaviour, client-centred therapy, goal-directed therapy; relationship therapies; emotional therapy; anger management counselling; therapies to enhance 'emotional intelligence'. On the face of it, such trends could be seen as evidence that the forces of *demedicalisation* are gaining the 'upper hand' in society, particularly as the concern for self and health moves out of the clinics and not only occupies community but apparently preoccupies individual biographies too. The underlying theme of the chapter is to consider what such developments hold for the dialectic between medicalisation and demedicalisation. This theme leads us to consider the relationship between the 'happiness and therapy industry' and broader social changes associated with high modernity, a concept first outlined in Chapter Three. The latter positions the 'happiness industry' as part of a much wider cultural shift in which relationships become medicalised through being increasingly mediated in terms of the personal, the psychological and the emotive, and less in terms of the collective bonds between people. The chapter concludes that the critics are surely correct in highlighting some of the darker sides to this industry and also the manipulative ways in which people's emotions and trust are part and parcel of the raw material of capitalist profits. Yet it is wrong to believe that individuals are duped by the self-help industry into being gullible users and believers of what it provides, because there is also evidence of a certain level of healthy scepticism and pragmatism pervading individuals' choices when it comes to their relationships with the self-help and happiness industry.

Chapter Six considers the present concern with obesity. We are often confronted by media and government reports that obesity is a key health concern facing society, and fast attaining the status of an epidemic. Obesity is portrayed as an unstoppable train, out of control and threatening to reverse the achievement of increased longevity in the developed world. How accurate are these claims? The chapter outlines the official definition of obesity and describes recent statistical trends that emerge from this definition, before drawing on the conceptual framework offered by discourse analysis to describe three competing discourses on obesity: *medical, social structural* and *social construction*. Each discourse illuminates key aspects of obesity while marginalising others. In this respect, the chapter considers how, on the one hand, the medical discourse offers key insights into obesity, but on the other hand, it serves to marginalise the significance of social structural factors central to obesity, while social structural causes of obesity tend to objectify obesity as a fact, and so tend to ignore or play down how obesity is socially constructed by a range of social factors, including both the medical and social discourses. The chapter concludes by arguing that all three discourses – medical, social structural and social construction – are crucial to a broader understanding of obesity and why it is a key issue in contemporary society, while also offering insights into the contested nature of the medicalisation of obesity in the wider context of late modernity.

During the 2000s there has also been an increasing concern with 'binge drinking'. The news and media coverage has shown a consistent preoccupation with negative images of anti-social, binge-drinking youth. The tabloid press has led the way with lurid stories about escalating incidents of binge drinking, now seen by some as the new 'British disease'. The UK government and the British Medical Association have expressed their growing concern with what they perceive to be an epidemic among binge-drinking youth. Chapter Seven evaluates binge drinking as a recent concept with multiple meanings. Drawing on evidence from a range of sources, including the media, health professionals and government, the chapter explains how each of these sources treats binge drinking as something objective, to be either medically cured or controlled. The chapter then examines the concept of moral panic as another way of approaching binge drinking, one that does not assume it is an objective fact outside of social meaning. Here we examine for whom drinking is a social problem to be medicalised, and we reflect on who is defining binge drinking and whose interests are served by these definitions. The chapter concludes that, if we embed the concept of 'binge drinking' in wider social structural changes affecting youth today, we can better articulate why the nature of binge drinking is both an objective reality and an object of social construction in a process that medicalises perceptions of 'youth' as a social problem that has its origin in wider social transformations that are adversely affecting the transition from youth to adulthood.

Questions for further reflection

1 Why is medicalisation sometimes difficult to define?
2 Select three examples of everyday issues that have been subjected to medicalisation.
3 In each example, explain who or what are the principal driving forces of medicalisation.

References

Allen, C.T., Fournier, S. and Miller, F. (2007) 'Brands and their meaning makers', in P. Curtis et al (eds) *Handbook of consumer psychology*, London: Psychology Press.

American Psychiatric Association (2000) *Diagnostic and statistical manual of mental disorders: DSM-IV-TR,* Washington: American Psychiatric Association, Task Force on DSM-IV.

Beck, U. (1992) *Risk society: Towards a new modernity*, London: Sage Publications.

Becker, H. (1963) *Outsiders*, New York, Free Press.

Berger, P.L. and Luckmann, T. (1991 [1967]) *The social construction of reality: A treatise in the sociology of knowledge*, London: Penguin.

Burr, V. (1995) *An introduction to social constructionism*, London: Routledge.

Conrad, P. (1992) 'Medicalization and social control', *Annual Review of Sociology*, vol 18, pp 209-32.

Douglas, M. (1970) *Purity and danger: An analysis of concepts of pollution and taboo*, London: Routledge.

Foucault, M. (1976) *The birth of the clinic: An archaeology of medical perception*, London: Tavistock.

Foucault, M. (2001) *Madness and civilization: A history of insanity in the age of reason* (2nd edn), London, Routledge.

Friedson, E. (1988) *Profession of medicine, a study of the sociology of applied knowledge*, Chicago: Chicago University Press.

Furedi, F. (2004) *Therapy culture: Cultivating vulnerability in an uncertain age*, London: Routledge.

Hebl, M.R. and Kleck, R.E. (2002) 'Virtually interactive: A new paradigm for the analysis of stigma', *Psychological Inquiry*, vol 13, no 2, pp 128–32.

Huxley, M. (2008) 'Space and government: governmentality and geography', *Geography Compass*, vol 2, no 5, pp 1635–58.

Manning, N. (2001) 'Psychiatric diagnosis under conditions of uncertainty: personality disorder, science and professional legitimacy', in J. Busfield (ed) *Rethinking the sociology of mental health*, Oxford: Blackwell.

Parsons, T. (1964 [1951]) *The social system*, New York: Free Press.

Romano, T.M. (2002) *Making medicine scientific: John Burdon Sanderson and the culture of Victorian science*, Baltimore, MD: Johns Hopkins University Press.

Senior, M. and Viveash, B. (1998) *Health and illness*, London: Macmillan.

Smith, M. (1998) *Social science in question*, London: Sage.

Szasz, T. (2007) *The medicalization of everyday life, selected essays*, Syracuse: Syracuse University Press.

Turner, B. (2008) *Body and society: Explorations in social theory* (3rd rev edn), London: Sage.

White, K. (2002) *Introduction to the sociology of health and illness*, London: Sage.

WHO (1994) *International statistical classification of diseases and related health problems.*

Zola, I.K. (1978) 'Medicine as an institution of social control: the medicalising of society', in D. Tuckett and J.M. Kaufert (eds) *Basic readings in medical sociology*, London: Tavistock Publications.

TWO

Medicine in modernity: a critical political economy

Medical practice sponsors sickness by reinforcing a morbid society that encourages people to become consumers of curative, preventative, industrial and environmental medicine … The patient in the grip of contemporary medicine is but one instance of mankind in the grip of its pernicious techniques … [which] … can be reversed only through the recovery of the will to self-care among the laity, and through the legal, political and institutional recognition of the right to care, which imposes limits on the professional autonomy of physicians. (Illich, 1987, pp 33–5)

Medicine had inherited the role of the healer priests …The conquest of polio and smallpox, the removal of parental fear that their children will die of pneumonia or diphtheria or tuberculosis before they reach adulthood and the many other successes are unequivocal and readily demonstrable. (Horrobin, 1978, pp 87–8)

… the medical profession has a dual function. One, needed under any mode of production, is to contribute to the care and cure of health and disease. The other function is the control function over the working class and the popular masses … These two functions do not exist side-by-side, but, rather the control function is done through the needed function … the controlling function could not take place unless there was a need for medicine and unless medicine was effective in resolving, at least partially, the problems of disease. (Navarro, 1978, p 242)

Introduction

It was earlier suggested that the sociology of medicine 'produces' medicalisation no less than medicine and the state produce it, albeit in very different ways. Professional sociologists produce medicalisation in the sense that they construct *conceptual contexts* or frames of reference through which medicine's expanding domain in society is given meaning and shape. In other words, we come to 'know' what medicalisation is in different ways which are shaped not only by what medicine does, but also by the ways in which sociologists *represent* medicalisation through particular conceptual lenses. We noted in the previous chapter that Parsons' original exploration of the formalisation of the 'sick role' was one of the first to move away from the biological presuppositions of 'sickness', to frame it as the outcome of negotiation between doctor and patient (Parsons, 1964). Parsons revealed how the doctor–patient relation draws on wider rules and values concerning health and illness, normal/abnormal, and in doing so brought to light the crucial role played by medicine as an institution of social order maintenance. In so doing, Parsons presents medicalisation in a certain light. In particular, he explains how, on the one hand, medical professionals serve the social order by legitimising the withdrawal of individuals from their social responsibilities to family and employers and exempting them from responsibility for their illness, while, on the other hand, patients accept their medical diagnosis and treatment and their responsibility to get well. Zola examined the expanding frontiers of medical influence in society: as a means of advice, scientific understanding and providing moral guidance over ostensibly non-medical matters (Zola, 1972). Zola extended this by helping to shed light on medicalisation as the blurring of the boundaries between medical and moral guidance over matters as diverse as birth control, obesity and physical exercise, influenced both by the power of medical professionals to impose meaning and by the apparent willingness of individuals to use the language of medicine when making sense of their daily experiences.

The over-arching conceptual framework within which both Parsons and Zola work is that of modernity. Modernity refers to the set of taken-for-granted beliefs about science, social order and the possibility of social progress. Modernity claims access to objective and universal truths about the nature of individuals, society and the natural environment. Individuals, society and nature are conceived as having relatively enduring natures and needs that manifest in regular patterns of behaviour which can be measured. The powers of human reason, applied through the sciences, are able to disclose the hidden laws of the natural and social worlds, and to use this information to regulate and master both worlds in the interests of bettering humanity. Modernity is defined in urban life by a distinct social ordering based around class divisions, in terms of the physical location of classes, housing status, health experience, occupational status, leisure pursuits and education. In fitting with the logic of modernity, the main institutions of the social welfare state sustain social order, in balance with maintaining individual freedom and the required conditions for wealth creation. In particular, what holds central stage within the state is the view that the welfare needs of individuals can be known, predicted and measured. Welfare needs, as a consequence, can be planned and administered by the state and by the array of professional institutions that adopt the basic assumptions of modernity. It is through this lens of modernity that Parsons and Zola constructed their respective contributions to an understanding of the role of medicine and the expanding logic of medical interventions in society.

While Parsons and Zola have rightly received ample attention in the sociological literature, relatively less attention has been given to the work of Illich and Marxism. In this chapter we draw on Illich's and Marxist approaches to medicine, to show how their different conceptualisations of modernity produce very different understandings of the role and purpose of medicine and the significance given to medicalisation. More specifically, as this chapter will demonstrate, by focusing on Illich and Marxism, one is better able to draw on theoretical perspectives which pay due attention to the specific *contradictions* and social *conflicts* central to the wider *political economy* within which medicine operates under conditions of modernity.

The term 'political economy' describes the analysis of forms of government related to the economy and public institutions, including political aspects of economic policy making (*Concise Oxford Dictionary*, 2003). For Sayer (2003, p 2), *critical political economy* refers to a critical inquiry into the normative foundations of the dominant governance of the economy and public institutions, with the aim of exposing the existence of 'avoidable suffering and disadvantage' and, by implication, revealing the 'possibility and desirability of alternatives'. One might add that a critical political economy ought also to account for the benefits and advantages, as it is rarely the case that dominant forms of governance simply impose themselves negatively upon society. Therefore, for the purposes of this chapter, a *critical political economy of medicine* is one which critically evaluates the dominant form of its organisation in relation to the wider economy, with a view to exposing its benefits as well as the 'existence of avoidable suffering and disadvantage' and highlighting possible alternatives.

Having established the basics of what is meant by critical political economy, this chapter will develop it in relation to an understanding of modern medicine. First it will provide an outline of Illich's critique of industrial medicine, as it emerges from the conflict–ridden power structures of 'industrial society' and then evaluate this critique in terms of how it helps us to understand the nature of modern medicine. The chapter then outlines the Marxist approach to medicine in capitalist society and provides critical commentary on the connections it seeks to establish between developments in how medicine is organised and the class relations and contradictions of modern capitalist society.

Specifically, the chapter explores and examines how:

- Illich provides a powerful and insightful critique of the negative power and influence of medicine in society, which accords very well with aspects of the evidence presented on systemic medical error, misapplication of drugs and the close influence of the pharmaceutical industry;
- Illich does not give due recognition to the positive contributions of medicine in the fight against disease and to increased health outlined earlier in this chapter;
- following Marx, the contradictory nature of medicine may be understood in terms of the limited autonomy that the medical profession has, combined with the functions it serves within the wider capitalist society;
- medical practice and its consequences are mediated by the definitions of health and illness inscribed within the capitalist economy and requirements for functionally productive labour, as well as by the requirement that use values and social needs, such as those for healthcare, either enhance or, at worst, do not set insurmountable limits to the requirements of the capitalist economy for profit;

- the medicalisation of society thesis needs to take account of capitalist relations, which both facilitate and present limits to the medicalisation of society.

Ivan Illich

Background

Illich was born in Vienna in 1926. He studied theology and philosophy at the Gregorian University in Rome and obtained a PhD in History at the University of Salzburg. He went to the United States in 1951, where he served as assistant pastor in an Irish–Puerto Rican parish in New York City. He rose to fame in the 1970s when he wrote a series of critical commentaries on the major institutions of the industrialised world, including education, transport and, perhaps most famously, medicine. He attempted to demonstrate how and why each of these institutions ended up working in ways that reversed its original purpose: for example, education becomes unthinking dogma and medicine ends up making you ill (Finger and Asún, 2001).

Illich's critique of medicine and other welfare institutions rested on a much wider critique of modern industrial society. The latter, he believed, caused the formal institutions of medicine and education to become corrupt and to malfunction, to the detriment of the people who relied on them most. Industrial society, he argued, dehumanised people, treating them like cogs in a bureaucratic machine. Industry deals with inputs and outputs and with efficiency and profits, and treats goods as commodities to be bought and sold in the marketplace (Illich, 1987). In this context, medicine, schools and healthcare institutions soon become *infected* by this industrial ethos. Firstly, bureaucratic institutions, and not the individuals they are supposed to serve, create needs and control satisfaction and, by so doing, turn the human being and her or his creativity into objects. 'This process undermines people – it diminishes their confidence in themselves and in their capacity to solve problems ... It kills convivial relationships. Bureaucracy colonizes life like a parasite or a cancer that kills creativity' (Finger and Asún, 2001, p 10). One example of this is when the NHS makes decisions about rationing healthcare and medical interventions. It does this through setting the different priorities and resources that ought to be given to one illness rather than another, based upon professional and managerial judgements of our needs. Secondly, bureaucratic society creates a layer of professionals and experts who redirect and reinterpret services and needs, such as schooling and healthcare, in their favour; so that their status and authority within the system grows.

> Experts and an expert culture always call for more experts. Experts also have a tendency to cartelise themselves by creating 'institutional barricades' – for example, proclaiming themselves gatekeepers – as well as by self-selecting themselves. Finally, experts control knowledge

production, as they decide what valid and legitimate knowledge is, and how its acquisition is sanctioned (Finger and Asún, 2001, p 10).

One stark example of this is how successful orthodox medicine has been in maintaining authority over what constitutes medical knowledge, over and above rival or 'alternative medicines' (an issue we consider in more depth in Chapter Three). Thirdly, services such as medicine, education and so on, become commodified, that is, treated in terms of production either for profit or as a source of cost containment by those who control them, and as something to be consumed by patients/customers. In the latter case, there is a growing tendency to expect to be 'perfectly healthy' and to treat illness as somehow not a part of human existence: that is to say, the commodification of a service leads to the patient or student becoming alienated from it, becoming objects of the service instead of the service meeting the more realistic, but specific and determinate, needs that we have a say in.

As Finger and Asún (2001, p 11) have commented, 'Illich is not against schools or hospitals as such, but once a certain threshold of institutionalization is reached, schools make people more stupid, while hospitals make them sick. And more generally, beyond a certain threshold of institutionalized expertise, more experts are counterproductive – they produce the counter effect of what they set out to achieve.'

In other words, institutions created to organise our health or education needs develop to the point where they become divorced from fulfilling those needs and begin to redefine their own rationale for existence: organisational needs take over and then contradict human needs, and so the original intention. For example, if learning is the original aim of education, bureaucratic organisations invert this aim to one of knowledge processing and rule following.

Illich's critique of medicine

Illich's central critique is that medicine causes clinical, social and cultural iatrogenesis. What follows is an overview of Illich's main argument as set out in his book *Limits to Medicine* (1976). All page references relate to this source.

Clinical iatrogenesis

> In the most narrow sense ..., includes only illnesses that would not have come about if sound professionally recommended treatment had not been applied ... In a more general and widely accepted sense, clinical iatrogenic disease comprises all clinical conditions for which remedies, physicians, or hospitals are the pathogens, or 'sickening agents'. I will call this plethora of therapeutic side-effects clinical iatrogenesis. (Illich, 1976, pp 26–7)

Illich argues that, historically, medicine has always had unwanted side effects; however, modern medicine has increased its powers of intervention to the point where the side effects become its defining characteristic: only malnutrition and war cause more human casualties than organised medicine (p 26). At the forefront of medicine's increasing powers are the mountain of drugs pumped out by the pharmaceuticals industry. Some of these drugs alleviate pain and suffering but this is a side effect of the profits they earn for the drugs industry and the power they give to the medical establishment who control distribution to the public.

> Some drugs are addictive, others mutilating, and others mutagenic ... in combination with food colouring or insecticides. In some patients, antibiotics alter the normal bacterial flora and induce a super infection, permitting more resistant organisms to proliferate and invade the host. Other drugs contribute to the breeding of drug-resistant strains of bacteria. (p 28)

In the above extract Illich mentions super infections and resistant organisms developing through the overuse of drugs such as antibiotics. This makes one think of the superbug MRSA, which is currently invading hospitals in the UK. MRSA, or methicillin-resistant staphylococcus aureus, first appeared in the 1960s but has now reached epidemic proportions in some hospitals in the UK. It has been estimated that hospital-acquired infections overall strike around 100,000 people each year in England, costing the NHS £1 billion (Andalo, 2005). According to the Department of Health (2004), MRSA is highly resistant to conventional antibiotics, making it extremely difficult to treat.

Illich goes on to argue that within formal healthcare institutions, underpinned as they are by the veneer of 'scientific detachment', the ethical and cultural implications of malpractice resulting from the nature of modern medicine become reduced to impersonal 'technical problems' and/or the result of 'random error' on the part of individuals. There is, in other words, no questioning by the media, or government or the medical establishment itself, of the fundamentals of biomedicine and its dominance in healthcare, because they are shielded by the veneer of 'scientific neutrality'. The response we get instead, argues Illich, is the growth of a litigation industry, replete with an army of law firms, standing in line to accrue profit from the misfortune of those on the receiving end of clinical iatrogenesis. While litigation may help to secure financial justice of sorts, it also leaves modern medicine intact and makes the 'maltreatment of patients an accepted routine' (p 31). Although Illich has the US healthcare and litigation industries in mind here, it can be argued that the situation is highly relevant to the UK today.

Finally, another crucial aspect of clinical iatrogenesis lies in the way that medicine 'sponsors sickness': by encouraging people to become consumers of the latest curative and preventative procedures, and through its 'certification of symptoms', medicine effectively exempts people from work, reinforcing a morbid society (p 33).

While Viagra and plastic surgery have their medical and social uses, as mass commodities for consumption, they are perfect contemporary examples of what, for Illich, would represent the acts of a morbid society, fascinated with illness and with staying virile and young, and unable or unwilling to accept the naturalness of growth, development and decline. We can now reach for those 'miracle cures': for Viagra to maintain youthful sexual performance; for pills to make our breasts bigger; or injections to strip away our body fat.

Social iatrogenesis

> When medical damage to individual health is produced by a socio-political mode of transmission, I will speak of 'social iatrogenesis', a term designating all impairments to health that are due precisely to those socio-economic transformations which have been made attractive, possible, or necessary by the institutional shape healthcare has taken. (p 40)

By social iatrogenesis, Illich refers to a situation whereby the professional autonomy of medicine to apply its specialist knowledge in the interests of patients becomes transformed into a radical monopoly over patient care. This radical monopoly seeks to marginalise the patient's own self-healing abilities and other ways of approaching healthcare – for example, complementary medicines. As such, more areas of life become medicalised. Births and deaths just as much as sickness become activities performed within formal healthcare institutions: 'homes become inhospitable to birth, sickness and death' (p 41). Using home birth as an example, women in the UK still have the right to a home birth, insofar as there are no laws forcing a woman to go into hospital. However, the health authority is not obliged to provide a home birth *service* (an attending midwife or doctor) to every woman who requests it. It is only where it is deemed to be 'clinically appropriate', that is, once medicine has given the go-ahead, that the NHS will support a woman who intends to give birth at home (Home Birth UK, 2001).

There is also the tendency to medicalise social issues. So, for example, a child who exhibits the following characteristics:

1 difficulty sustaining attention
2 impulse control or inhibition
3 excessive activity
4 difficulty following rules and instructions
5 excessive variability in responses to situations, particularly doing work,

can be interpreted by medicine as having a medical condition with genetic/biological origins, putting aside the possibility of poor parenting skills, social deprivation or anything fussily social such as the result of the stresses and strains of coping with a 24-hour consumer society. Yet in the 1910s this 'condition' was called 'morbid defect of moral control'; in the 1960s it was then changed to 'hyperkinetic reaction of childhood'; and in the 1980s it got a further makeover to 'attention deficit disorder', before finally taking its present medical label of 'attention deficit hyperactivity disorder' (ADHD) (Anastopoulos, 2001). Apparently the hyperactive element of the 'condition' went unnoticed in the 1980s.

Illich's point would perhaps be that childbirth is a human event rather than a medical problem, and that child behavioural syndromes such as ADHD are largely social problems that result from living in an industrial society. Thus, we should refrain from reducing them to biological inevitabilities, primarily amenable to medical treatment.

Social iatrogenesis also refers to the redefinition (or reduction) of broader social issues and exploitative relationships to individual medical problems, referring to how medicine helps to refocus attention away from the wider social ills of society and redefine them instead to an individual illness. As Illich reflects, medicine

> serves to legitimise social arrangements into which many people do not fit. It labels the handicapped [*sic*] as unfit and breeds ever new categories of patients. People who are angered, sickened, and impaired by their industrial labour and leisure can escape only into a life under medical supervision and are thereby seduced or disqualified from political struggle for a healthier world. (p 43)

An individual picks up her inhaler from the GP for her asthma condition on the way home to her damp, under-heated house; the retired mineworker picks up his medication to ease his silicosis-induced coughing fits; the bronchitis sufferer renews her prescription after making her daily payment into the coffers of multinational tobacco companies. In each case medicine is, according to Illich, unwittingly or otherwise, redirecting the focus from broader social issues, such as the conditions of employment in coal mining, onto the individual.

Social iatrogenesis also manifests with the medicalisation of all stages of the life cycle. Life's cultural rituals are medicalised:

> from the crib to the terminal ward, each age-cohort is conditioned by a milieu that defines health for those whom it segregates. ... For rich and for poor, life is turned into a pilgrimage through check-ups and clinics back to the ward where it started. Life is thus reduced to a 'span', to a statistical phenomenon which, for better or for worse, must be institutionally planned and shaped. This lifespan is brought into existence with the prenatal check, when the doctor decides if and how the foetus shall be born, and it will end with a mark on a chart ordering resuscitation suspended. (p 79)

Cultural iatrogenesis

Cultural iatrogenesis completes Illich's circle depicting medicine's domination of the modern human soul. Whereas clinical iatrogenesis is concerned with the systematisation of medical malpractice and social iatrogenesis with the extension of medicine into areas of social life, cultural iatrogenesis depicts a world in which individuals have been sapped of the ability to self-heal and the confidence to live with less than perfect health: they have become passive receptacles of the power of biomedicine! For Illich, being in 'good health' means being able to cope with reality, enjoy success and feel 'alive in pleasure and in pain' (p 128). Each culture has specific ways of expressing health, illness, pain, impairment; in short, it has its own unique 'art of suffering'. It is in this cultural context that one can experience a 'healthy' relationship with one's body and with one's bodily ills and strengths: 'how he relates to the sweetness and the bitterness of reality and how he acts towards others whom he perceives as suffering, as weakened, or as anguished determine each person's sense of his own body, and with it, his health' (p 129). However, modern medicine's domination of suffering, its 'domineering moral enterprise' to enact a 'war against suffering', 'undermines the ability of individuals to face their reality, express their own values, and to accept inevitable and often irremediable pain and impairment, decline, and death' (p 128).

There are many examples of what is implied here by Illich. The older person who is under continual observations and a battery of invasive medical tests for loss of weight, related to natural decline; or the person who defers to the doctor's diagnosis even though it may not 'feel correct'. In other words, argues Illich, we become estranged from our own feelings and self-healing powers, and so place these powers in the hands of others.

Evidence in support of Illich's critique of medicine

We noted earlier that the sociology of medicine is part of the overall production of medicalisation. It can be argued that Illich also plays his part in representing medicine in a certain way. In particular, Illich represents medicalisation as a totalising and wholly negative influence through the three related forms of iatrogenesis – clinical, social and cultural. Illich's critique can be used to galvanise evidence in support of this conceptualisation of medicine. Later we will see that Marxism provides a different way of knowing medicalisation. First we need to explore the evidence that supports and contradicts Illich's central thesis.

If we accept some of the findings over recent decades, then medicine certainly poses a considerable threat to our health. It has been estimated that in the US in 1974, 2.4 million unnecessary surgeries were performed, resulting in 11,900 deaths at an annual cost of $3.9 billion. By 2001 the figure had risen to 7.5 million unnecessary surgical procedures, resulting in 37,136 deaths at a cost of $122 billion (Null et al, 2003). A study of New York hospitals carried out in 1990 found that almost 4% of admissions were associated with an error and that 14% of patients who experienced an error died – partly because of the error. The *British Medical Journal* calculated that if the same error rate applied in British hospitals, then 300,000 patients each year would experience an error and 45,000 would die, partly because of it (*British Medical Journal*, 2000).

Evidence drawn from the UK is equally supportive of Illich's critique. For example, it has been estimated that the third largest cause of death after cancer and heart disease is medical error. It is estimated that 300,000 patients every year experience a medical error. Of these, 70% (200,000) suffer no permanent damage and 16% suffer serious and permanent damage to their health. The remaining 14% (40,000) die – 'the equivalent of two jumbo jets crashing every week' (*Sunday Times*, 1999).

One other indication of escalating medical harm is the rise of litigation. A report by the Organisation for Economic Cooperation and Development (OECD, 2003) highlighted the enormous cost of clinical errors and revealed that the NHS faced a bill of almost £6 billion in cases of medical negligence claims it expected to lose. On average, a case takes five years to resolve, with in excess of 20,000 cases outstanding at any one time. By value, 80% of claims in the report were for cerebral palsy caused by surgical and clinical negligence. Moreover, there had been a dramatic rise in the rate of claims made against the NHS, with a rise of 72% in the claims made by patients between 1990 and 1998 (OECD, 2003). However, according to the OECD, the above claims were the tip of the iceberg (OECD, 2003), if we also consider that many grievances never get to the stage of an official claim.

According to a House of Commons report in 2005, *The National Patient Safety Agency*, in excess of half a million errors were made on patients in acute NHS hospitals each year. The report pointed out that 'most incidents resulted in no harm to the patient but in 840 cases the patient died'. Incidents included unsafe medication practices with anti-coagulants, exposure of patients with tracheotomy to risk, patients wrongly identified for blood transfusions they did not require, and unnecessary X-rays and surgery.

As one *British Medical Journal* editorial (2000, p 730) acknowledged:

> Medication error – wrong drug, wrong dose, wrong route of administration, wrong patient, wrong time – is the most common single preventable cause of patient injury. When all sources of error are added up the likelihood that a mishap will injure a patient in hospital is at least 3% and probably much higher. This is a serious public health problem when one considers that a typical airline handles customers' baggage at a far lower error rate than we handle the administration of drugs to patients, it is also an embarrassment.

However, the *BMJ* also points out that medical errors cannot simply be blamed on individual blunders, but are more often the outcome of systemic weaknesses in the way medical and healthcare organisations operate. Therefore, while individuals are often blamed (rightly or wrongly in some cases), most are latent errors, or errors 'waiting to happen', arising from poorly designed processes and systems of care (*British Medical Journal*, 2000).

Alongside systemic error is the argument that medicine was never the principal reason for the longer life expectancy and better quality of health in the first place! In this respect, the argument that 'big medical' advances paved the way towards lower mortality rates historically between 1850 and1950 has come under increasing question from those who argue that the lower mortality rates were down to other factors, such as better diet, better sewerage and higher standards of living. Medicine, it is argued, played a marginal role in this achievement (McKeown, 1976). Later critics support this claim by referring to evidence that increased spending on medicine and healthcare has no necessary positive correlation with lower mortality rates or reduction of disease. For example, the OECD would appear to make this case when noting that, although the US spent 5% more on medicine and healthcare than Canada and 10% more than the UK, there was no discernible difference in the health of the populations covered (OECD, 2003).

Medical misuse of drugs

Research by Null et al (2003) indicates the extent of harm caused by the misuse of drugs in the health industry. They reveal a situation where the unnecessary use of antibiotics and mood-altering drugs has become a serious health concern. For example, Null et al found that a *New England Journal of Medicine* study showed that an

> alarming one-in-four patients suffered observable side effects from the more than 3.34 billion prescription drugs filled in 2002 … The drugs with the worst record of side effects were the SSRIs, the NSAIDs, and calcium-channel blockers. Reuters also reported that prior research has suggested that nearly 5% of hospital admissions – over 1 million per year – are the result of drug side effects. But most of the cases are not documented as such. The study found one of the reasons for this failure: in nearly two-thirds of the cases, doctors couldn't diagnose drug side effects or the side effects persisted because the doctor failed to heed the warning signs.

They further suggested that

> a whole generation of antidepressant users has resulted from young people growing up on Ritalin. Medicating youth and modifying their emotions must have some impact on how they learn to deal with their feelings. They learn to equate coping with drugs and not their inner resources. As adults, these medicated youth reach for alcohol, drugs, or even street drugs, to cope … Today's marketing of mood-modifying drugs, such as Prozac or Zoloft, makes them not only socially acceptable but almost a necessity in today's stressful world.

Over-medication dominates medical procedures. It is estimated that over 3 million pounds (in weight!) of antibiotics are used every year on humans. This amount is enough to give the population of the US – 284 million – 10 teaspoons each of pure antibiotics per year. Yet 90% of upper respiratory infections, including children's ear infections, are viral, and antibiotics don't treat viral infection. And it is claimed that more than 40% of antibiotics (about 50 million prescriptions) were inappropriate (Null et al, 2003).

Of course, similar issues arise in the UK and Europe too. The House of Commons Select Committee on the Pharmaceutical Industry in the UK (2005) diplomatically pointed out to the pharmaceutical industry that 'the inappropriate or excessive use of medicines can cause distress, ill-health, hospitalisation and even death'. According to the Select Committee, 'adverse drug reactions are responsible for about 5% of all admissions to hospitals in the UK'. Indeed, the consumption of medication has increased year on year during the 2000s, and in 2005 accounted for 12% of the entire NHS budget. In 1993 the cost of prescribing drugs was £3.1 billion and by 2003 it had risen to £7.5 billion! The disadvantages noted by the House of Commons Select Committee were: increased medicalisation, enshrined in the philosophy of 'a pill for every ill'; and increased exposure to the risk of drug-induced harm to patients (House of Commons Select Committee on the Pharmaceutical Industry in the UK, 2005).

Drug companies are immensely powerful corporations, both economically and politically. As the Association of the British Pharmaceutical Industry (ABPI) reminds us, pharmaceuticals are a multi-billion pound industry, accounting for £184 billion worth of global sales each year. The biggest company is the US giant Pfizer, with sales annually of £29 billion, and the second biggest global company is the UK giant GlaxoSmithKline, with annual sales of £19 billion (ABPI, 2004). According to one source, through the Pharmaceutical Price Regulation Scheme (PPRS) the British lobby for the industry has secured a healthy return on profits, from sales to the NHS, of between 17% and 21% of capital invested (Socialist Health Association, 2005). Such a guaranteed rate of return is very lucrative and places the pharmaceutical industry in an enviable position relative to other industries – possibly one reason why it now employs more workers in the UK than the manufacturing sector!

The power of the pharmaceutical industry includes marketing to consumers through mass advertising of over-the-counter drugs, as well as canvassing general practitioners (GPs) in order to generate sales of prescribed drugs. It has been noted by Watkins et al (2003) that GPs who report weekly contact with drug representatives are more likely to express views that will lead to unnecessary prescribing than those who report less frequent contact. Moreover, when new drugs became available, GPs who see drug representatives at least weekly were more likely, as their first course of action, to prescribe them for a few patients and monitor the results. In addition, GPs who see drug representatives most often tend to be those who are isolated from their colleagues (single-handed practitioners and those uninvolved in GP training) and to work in deprived areas.

Lax controls at the Department of Health, allowing pharmaceutical companies to have increasing influence over the public and the medical profession, have led to over-prescribing by doctors and an unhealthy reliance on medicines by the public (Kmietowicz, 2005).

The benefits of modern medicine

While there is a great deal of evidence in support of Illich's critique of medicine, medicine also produces immense benefits which are hard to explain within his iatrogenic conceptual framework. We don't have to search far into our own experiences to acknowledge these benefits. For example, if we have the misfortune to break a leg or fracture a wrist we are all appreciative of the expertise of radiographers and doctors in using their medical expertise to locate and relieve the immediate pain, and accurately diagnose the nature of the break to speed our rehabilitation. It is worth remembering, too, that as recently as the 1960s a person suffering from heart or lung disease, chronic hip joint problems, kidney and liver failure, and so on, would have been incurable and would have expected to live a life of chronic illness or to experience an untimely death. Today, however, medical breakthroughs in these areas do at least ensure the possibility of recovery and a longer life (Russell, 1979). Moreover, the 20th century has witnessed a series of advances in medicine that have had beneficial outcomes for society. Some of humanity's major killers, in the form of infectious diseases, have been either cured or curbed by scientific advances in medicine. Examples include:

- the first magic bullet, Salvarsan 606 in 1909, cured syphilis;
- the discovery in 1932 of sulphonamides – a group of drugs that cured many infectious diseases, such as pneumonia;
- the discovery in 1929 of penicillin, which, by 1943, was a usable drug killing a wide variety of bacteria – still the most common antibiotic.

The availability of a wide variety of drugs to treat everything from cancer to mental illness and AIDS suggests that medicine has gone from strength to strength (Porter, 1999, p 3). Medical advances in surgery have resulted in better and safer anaesthetics; allowed longer operations; produced drugs to combat infection; allowed the possibility of more complex surgical procedures. Blood banks, established in the 1940s, also allow easy transfusion of blood. Instead of being merely antiseptic (germs killed on or near the open wound), surgery became aseptic (entire operating theatre kept germ free). Moreover, technological progress led to the development of X-ray machines from 1896, which allowed surgeons to see inside the body; and, more recently, to ECG machines, which can measure heart activity; lasers and ultrasound techniques, which have meant less invasive operations; and heart and lung machines, which keep the body going during transplant surgery (Kevles, 1997).

Medical advances have been made in other areas too. The medical understanding of nutrition has improved the quality of our lives. For example, advances in knowledge about the balance between the intake of fat, carbohydrates and protein in the diet, combined with the discovery of a series of vaccinations against air- and water-borne infectious diseases, such as smallpox and typhoid, as well as recognition of the importance of hygiene, eventually became the cornerstone of the Victorian public health movement. All have played a central role in decreasing the mortality rate for young and old alike (Sargent, 2003).

At the same time, it wasn't too long ago that diabetes was a major killer. Dodson (1998) estimated that five in every 1,000 of the human population are affected by the severe form of this disease, and about twice as many again by the milder form. Modern medical intervention has meant that diabetes is no longer a life-threatening condition. As Dodson reflects, 'The discovery of insulin and the demonstration that its injection could control blood sugar levels and give diabetics life, was one of the great moments in medicine, and a remarkable story of human character and the accidents that are so important in research' (Dodson, 1998).

Cutler (2004) also reminds us how cardiovascular disease has fallen, by roughly 50% in the US since 1950, from 800 per 100,000 to 350 per 100,000. Similar falls are evidenced across the West, including in the UK. Cutler argues that medical intervention is a significant factor in this reduction (Cutler, 2004, p 15). Likewise, medical intervention in the area of incubator and respiratory technology has dramatically lowered the mortality rate of low birth-weight infants, from five deaths in every 20 in 1950 to one death in every 20 today (Cutler, 2004, p 18).

More recently, computerised tomography (CT) scanning and magnetic resonance imaging (MRI) have increased the capacity to scan the brain more precisely for suspected encephalitis and multiple sclerosis, and have several important orthopaedic applications involving the spine, knees and hips. MRI can also be usefully applied to cases of suspected spinal cord compression, which often results from spinal tumours or from slipped disks (Feeney, 1996; Emsley and Feeney, 2007).

If we take all the above advances together, and others besides, we can draw the conclusion that each has played a major role in the increased life expectancy we have come to take for granted in the UK. As the OECD report on *Health data* (2003) observed, most OECD countries have enjoyed large gains in life expectancy over the past 40 years, thanks to improvements in living conditions, public health intervention and medical care. According to this report, life expectancy in the UK, at 78.5 years, was 0.7% higher than the OECD average. The infant mortality rate had also fallen dramatically over the same period of time, standing at 5.3 deaths per 1,000 live births.

Critical reflection on Illich in light of the evidence

Illich presents a powerful indictment of medicine's negative impact on society. The strength of his approach lies in his ability to integrate medicine into the values and relations of industrial society to present an over-arching account of how the power of medicine relates to developments in industrial society. Illich offers a critique that combines clinical, cultural and social processes and how each is affected by medicine in different ways; and also how the negative effects on each are the very source of medical power over populations. For example, Illich reveals how clinical side effects actually increase the demand for medicine; and how the cultural impact of medicine pacifies populations and so enables medicine to deepen its authority to apparently 'know the body' better than the individual. However, Illich's over-arching critique cannot, as is argued, adequately explain the benefits that are also inherent features of medical science.

Illich's representations of medicalisation tend to ignore or seriously play down the ability of individuals to resist the persuasive powers of medicine and adapt and reinterpret those powers to their own ends, in either limiting the scope of medicalisation or shaping medical encounters towards social models of health. Ironically, Illich's critique of medicine did form part of an intellectual and political critique of the social welfare state, which was eventually to be dominated by the New Right and led to the shift in government policy over recent decades, away from public administration and towards the market, individual responsibility and free choice (Jones, in Davies et al, 1999, p 14; Fitzpatrick, 2000, pp 139–40). Yet it was not Illich's intention to promote *market individualism*. Illich's critique of bureaucracy and professional power does *imply* the need for the resurgence of a more self-autonomous and reflective population, but not necessarily that envisaged by adherents of a free market ideology.

More crucially, perhaps, Illich's critical representations of medicine leave no space from which resistance might conceivably arise: Illich may hope for individuals to resist the 'industrial machine' and related medical bureaucracy that are thought to be fundamental to modernity, but he offers no theoretical framework to explain the material basis of this resistance. The following chapter will discuss in more detail the rise to prominence of self-help movements and the blossoming of interest in alternative forms of medicine, which have been presented as evidence of the partial *demedicalisation* of society within the broader framework of late modernity. Although Illich is sometimes cited as a precursor of the latter, his reflections on medicine are somewhat omniscient, drawing strength only from their insertion within 'the industrial machine' of modernity. This leaves little intellectual space for situating reflexive, critical individuals.

Illich also ignores the extent to which the medical profession is willing to critically engage with the negative aspects of medical practice. Yet a cursory glance at in-house medical journals such as, for example, the *British Medical Journal* reveals a healthy sceptical and critical attitude towards some of the more outlandish claims made on behalf of medicine. This would seem to cast doubt on the assumption that medical dominance is omnipotent and on the outcome of its relative professional and scientific autonomy from the wider capitalist society.

In summary, while Illich's representations of medicine within the context of modern industrial society provide a powerful and persuasive understanding of the hazards of medicine, he is largely silent on the beneficial impact it has had on society. However, the hazards and benefits of medical interventions appear to be inherent in the development of modern medicine. This suggests another representation of medicalisation, one in which medicine in industrial society does not play the role of an omnipotent social force in promoting medicalisation as a negative tour de force which is apparently impervious to human resistance. To discover such a view, in the remainder of this chapter we evaluate Marxist representations of modern medicine, and address the question of what critical political economy of medicine Marxism produces in order to represent the contradictory nature of modern medicine.

Marxist political economy of medicine in capitalist society

To understand the Marxist approach to modern medicine we must first explain the foundation of the latter in Marx's general critique of capitalism. For Marx, modernity was too general a term to describe modern society because it omitted what makes it specific: class struggle and the accumulation of capital. Marx represented superstructural institutions such as medicine and education in terms of the limits and opportunities presented by the wider capitalist industrial society of which they are part (Marx, 1954). Hence the representation of medicine, and indeed the tensions and ambiguities involved in the medicalisation of society, are to be located within Marx's conceptual framework for understanding capitalist relations. In this respect, Marx argued that in industrial capitalist society the production of capital (basically the profitable accumulation of money) is central to why we produce health and wealth (Marx, 1954). The driving force of capital accumulation is that of class conflict between capitalist and worker. The emphasis on class conflict is another key difference between Marx and Illich. Illich recognised the centrality of business interests, money making and profits, but did not prioritise class conflict as the central driving force; instead, for Illich, industrial and organisational bureaucracy and professional power were the source of power and control in society. However, according to the Marxist emphasis on capital accumulation and class struggle, the role of medicine is to be understood as being engulfed by the struggle between these two contending classes and, moreover, the source of medicine's contradictory nature (as both beneficial and hazardous) can be understood as deriving from this state of affairs. To grasp this, we need to first explain how medicine develops and functions in relation to class struggle and then to consider medicine's ambiguous nature as a commodity and how this ambiguity facilitates spaces of resistance for reflexive individuals and medicine as a practice.

With reference to class struggle, Marxist perspectives maintain that there are many classes in modern capitalist society but that the two most important classes for determining the pace and direction of social change are capitalists, who own and control 'capital' (money, wealth, technology, land and so on, which is used as a source of investment to make profits), and a working class, who own only their ability to work and the wages and savings which result from work (Edgell, 1993). The two classes are in a conflict with each other, patterned by repulsion and attraction. Each class requires the other to prosper (the capitalist requires the worker to work to make goods and services that can be sold for profit, while the worker requires to be employed by the capitalist for the income necessary to maintain living standards). However, despite this unity of interests, the classes are repelled by each other; workers produce and consume goods and services for their *social use*, whereas capitalists tend to approach the same goods and services as, primarily, something to be produced and sold for a profit. So, for workers it is the social usefulness derived from what is produced and consumed that ius important, while for capitalists the good or service produced is a commodity whose principal measure of usefulness is how much profit its sale will yield (Wright, 1978).

Turning to medicine, the class struggle produces specific functions for medicine. Capitalists require (1) workers healthy enough to be put to work to make profits and (2) medicine that provides ideological justification for the social inequalities between rich and poor that capitalism produces. Medicine must also cater for the needs of organised workers; workers in capitalism struggle to gain access to meaningful medicine and healthcare (Navarro, 1976). For example, medicine may have some autonomy in pursuit of power and dominance, but it is very much circumscribed within the limits imposed by the class struggle between capital and labour (Edgell, 1993). Medicine's autonomy is limited by a system in which the management and direction of services towards healing and the interests of ensuring the profitability of the capitalist economy are often in conflict but have to be resolved. The dominant form of medicine in the West – biomedicine – provides key functional roles for capital. The first is that biomedicine narrows down the definition of health in terms of absence of illness, and of illness itself in terms of variation from a state of relative able-bodiedness, that is, whether one is fit enough to work or, if unemployed, whether one has the potential to work (Doyal and Pennell, 1979). Although always the subject of resistance and counter-definitions based on the social model of health, this narrow definition is more amenable to enabling the welfare system to keep a tight track on the unemployed, the 'idle' and the sick. As well as providing legitimate definitions (in terms of system requirements) of a functionally healthy workforce, the discipline this has on workers and the potential constraining effect it has on welfare spending have a positive effect on the profitability of the capitalist system (Navarro, 1978).

Second, medicine individualises the source of illness by relating it either to the personal or cultural habits of the individual or to their biology (Navarro, 1986). This diminishes the impact that the wider capitalist economy has on the social and natural environment and on health and illness as a result of rapid industrial growth driven by the profit motive. Marxists would point to the trend towards health promotion in public health, where the emphasis is on the individual to take responsibility for becoming healthier and to be self-vigilant against the threat of disease. Third, as Illich also draws out, biomedicine has close ties with the private sector through the pharmaceutical industry, for which healthcare systems such as the NHS represent a significant market for the consumption of drugs and medical technology, and thus a significant source of profits (Navarro, 1986).

Turning to medicine as a commodity, as mentioned earlier, Marxists point out that capitalism is a society focused on accumulating capital (profit in the form of money), and therefore the central feature of this society is that the goods and services created (ideally anything and everything from consumer durables to cancer research) have as their central driving force the creation of monetary profit. (Marxists argue that it is almost as if useful things like cancer research are a by-product of the drive to increase money profits rather than having the main rationale of progressing towards finding a cure for cancer.) Cancer research and consumer durables are hardly ethically reciprocal as vehicles for profit. Marx also argued that some activities are not so easily reducible to commodities to be produced for sale and profit (Marx, 1954), in which case capitalist society is in a constant struggle to transform such goods, services and needs into commodities.

Commodification is 'that process by which an object or social practice acquires an exchange value or market-centered meaning ... involving the gradual entry of market logic to the various elements that constitute the object or social practice under consideration' (Giulianotti, 2002, p 26). Marx and Engels argued that commodification was never, as it were, a 'done deal', but in flux as part of an open-ended class struggle (Marx and Engels, 1998). Therefore objects, practices, relations in capitalist society (such as medicine and healthcare) are always in flux, always becoming commodities (medicine and health as something to be produced and consumed for a price and profit), but never fully commodified, because they are also becoming use values (healthcare and good health as an intrinsically human goal, whatever the monetary cost); likewise, they are becoming use values, but rarely develop their full capacity as use values (a situation we have outlined earlier when recording the benefits and hazards of medicine) because they are also becoming commodities designed to be sold with either profit or cost minimisation uppermost in mind. In other words, Marx would argue that the struggle and resistance associated with economic rationality is taking over areas such as medical and healthcare ethics and is inherent to the process of commodification (Navarro, 1978).

Polanyi (1957), who applied a very similar argument to Marx's, but extended it in terms of its relevance to our subject matter, also understood the limits to economic rationality which underpinned the commodity structure of the economy, arguing 'that the most basic human characteristic – the need to relate to other humans, to feel part of a larger community' (McQuaig, 2005, p 2) offers natural limits to commodification. Consumer goods may appear to be natural commodities, but Polanyi's point was that activities such as health and medicine are really 'fictitious commodities', by which he meant there is a greater awareness that education and health, for example, are vital human endeavours, rather than objects that we produce for profit and consume for pleasure, even though they are often seen in this way. The term 'fictitious commodities' draws attention to a struggle between economy and society in capitalism, and specifically to the stripping away of a community asset or community need (such as medicine) from its wider social relations and its reinsertion within a market-mediated activity where business motives dominate, corrupt and distort the community asset (Polanyi, 1957).

The NHS is a case in point. In the NHS, market imperatives of costing and maximising resources are imposed externally by the pharmaceutical industry and by working to the budgetary constraints and audit controls imposed by government, and internally through reorganisation during the 2000s, which has seen the greater involvement of the private healthcare sector and creation of internal markets between hospitals, GPs and primary care. To this extent one can say that the NHS is becoming increasingly *commodified* (instrumental rational, calculative motivations are invading medical and healthcare decisions and practices). Set against this is the popular notion of healthcare as a universal need, free at the point of use, a powerful non-market sentiment in opposition to commodification. In consequence, commodification is a struggle, not a fact of life, and medicine as an institution is caught in the middle of this struggle, trying to come to terms with balancing costs and economic efficiencies alongside quality of healthcare as a universal human need.

The combined effects of medicine's functional role in the class struggle and the central position it has in the struggle waged over the commodification of medicine and healthcare sets serious limits to the *professional power of medicine over society*. Medicine mediates rather than dictates. Medicine expresses the conflicting interests of capitalist and worker. This is not to say that medicine does not have its own institutional power base. Quite the opposite: the conflict that medicine mediates also provides spaces of resistance, as indicated above in the discussion of commodification. The medical profession has its own internal rules and ethics of practice that it must attempt to uphold, and these will have an effect on just how far medicine bows to the wider societal functions it has to meet. There is plenty of autonomy for professional status building in an attempt to exert some control over the direction in which the medical profession wishes to advance. As reflected upon earlier (and contrary to Illich) the *British Medical Journal* is representative of a critical and reflexive medical profession, albeit one constrained by the wider demands/functional needs of society, but also able to be critical about whether those needs or functions should be adhered to, and in whose interests.

As Horrobin (1978, p 86) points out, Illich's critique of medicine is 'reasonably accurate but his refusal to recognise that most of the critical material he has assembled comes from medical sources and that much of the work has already been done by doctors themselves [suggests that] Illich is not such a lone prophet as he imagines himself to be.'

Moreover, Marxists might argue that their accounts of the open-ended struggle over the commodity status of medicine offer an explanation for what we described earlier as the emergence of critical lay perspectives, displaying their ability and willingness to resist the persuasive powers of a medicine heavily influenced by capitalism and to adapt and reinterpret those powers to their own ends. In this respect, the many user and/or self-help medical and health-related campaign groups, from diabetics societies to Asperger's Syndrome associations, would seem to conflict with images of a passive and docile population. The blossoming of interest in alternative forms of medicine, fuelled by an information-rich society, would appear to contradict Illich's vision of cultural docility and imply the existence of a more savvy and complex modern health consumer. The Marxist critical economy of medicine would claim to go beyond Illich in explaining how and why the power of medicine remains, while the modern health consumer is also able to reflect critically and selectively on the health claims of the biomedical industry before deciding to consume what it has to 'offer' or reject it for a range of complementary and alternative medicines.

Marxism has often been accused of reducing culture and politics and the actions of social agents to economic structures and laws. In some readings of Marxism this may be accurate. Yet, as the above account of commodification – as an open-ended struggle that social actors can pursue and resist – makes clear, the power of human agency to affect social change is inherent in Marxism. Nevertheless, by prioritising social class conflict and a class perspective, the Marxist approach to medicine tends to leave unexamined gender and ethnic perspectives on the nature of modern medicine. This is perhaps less of a criticism of Marxist approaches to medicine per se, and instead more of a recognition that such approaches, as well as Illich's critique, have their respective limits and strengths.

Conclusion

We began this chapter by outlining Illich's powerful and insightful critique of the negative consequences of medicine in society, which accords very well with aspects of the evidence presented with respect to systemic medical error, misapplication of drugs and the close influence of the pharmaceutics industry. Yet it was also argued that Illich fails to give adequate recognition to the positive contributions medicine has made to the fight against disease and the promotion of population-wide health. The chapter has also considered medicalisation from the standpoint of the Marxist approach to medicine, that what is crucial in Illich's omission is his misunderstanding of medicine's role in industrial capitalist society. Evidence of the benefits and shortcomings of medicine that we considered in the course of this chapter tends to lend support to a theory more able to capture medicine as contradictory in its effects on individuals and on society as a whole. Moreover, this contradictory effect may be understood in terms of the limited autonomy the medical profession actually experiences, combined with the functions it serves within the wider capitalist society. In this respect it could be argued that the Marxist approach offers more scope than Illich's critique of medicine. As the chapter went on to argue, medical practice and its consequences are mediated by definitions of health and illness that are inscribed within the capitalist economy and the requirements for functionally productive labour, as well as by the requirement that use values and social needs, such as those for healthcare, either enhance or, at worst, do not set insurmountable limits to the requirements of the capitalist economy for profit.

Questions for further reflection

1 Search the media for three newspaper articles that offer support for Illich's critique of medicine.

2 Discuss whether or not you feel the benefits of modern medicine outweigh the negatives.

3 Explain why Marxist approaches conclude that medicine has contradictory consequences for society.

References

ABPI (Association of the British Pharmaceutical Industry) (2004) *Sales for top twenty drug companies* (www.obpri.org.uk).

Anastopoulos, A.D. (2001) *Assessing attention-deficit/hyperactivity disorder: Topics in social psychiatry* (1st edn), New York: Springer,

Andalo, D. (2005) 'MRSA the issue explained', *Guardian*, 22 March.

British Medical Journal (2000) Editorial: 'Let's talk about error. Leaders should take responsibility for mistakes', vol 320, no 18, p 730.

Concise Oxford Dictionary (2003) (www.encyclopedia.com/doc/1O86-politicaleconomy.html).

Cutler, D.M. (2004) 'Are the benefits of medicine worth what we pay for it?' Fifteenth Annual Herbert Lourie Memorial Lecture on Health Policy (www-cpr.maxwell.syr.edu/pbriefs/pb27.pdf).

Davies, C., Findlay, L. and Bullman, A. (1999) *Changing practices in health and social care*, London: Sage.

Department of Health (2004) *Towards cleaner hospitals and lower rates of infection*, London: Department of Health.

Dobson, G. (1998) 'Insulin and diabetes', Mill Hill Essays, National Institute for Medical Research (www.nimr.mrc.ac.uk/millhillessays/1998/diabetes.htm).

Doyal, L. and Pennell, I. (1979) *The political economy of health*, London: Pluto Press.

Edgell, S. (1993) *Class*, London: Routledge.

Emsley J.W. and Feeney, J. (2007) 'Forty years of progress in nuclear magnetic resonance spectroscopy', *Progress in Nuclear Magnetic Resonance Spectroscopy*, vol 50, no 4, 30 July, pp 179-98.

Feeney, J. (1996) *Magnetic resonance imaging: A window into the human body*, National Institute for Medical Research (www.nimr.mrc.ac.uk/millhillessays/1996/mri.htm).

Finger, M. and Asún, J. M. (2001) *Adult education at the crossroads: Learning our way out*, London: Zed Books.

Fitzpatrick, M. (2000) *The tyranny of health: Doctors and the regulation of lifestyle*, London: Routledge.

Giulianotti, R. (2002). 'Supporters, followers, fans and flaneurs: a taxonomy of spectator identities in football', *Journal of Sport and Social Issues*, vol 26, no 1, pp 25–46.

Home Birth UK (2001) *Home births in the UK* (www.homebirth.org.uk).

Horrobin, D.F. (1978) *Medical hubris. A reply to Ivan Illich*, London: Churchill Livingstone.

House of Commons Select Committee on the Pharmaceutical Industry in the UK (2005) *The influence of the pharmaceutical industry, Fourth Report of Session 2004–5*, vol 1 (April).

House of Commons (2005) *The National Patient Safety Agency*, London: The Stationery Office.

Illich, I. (1976) *Limits to medicine*, London: Marion Boyars.

Illich, I. (1987) *Towards a history of need*, Berkeley, CA: Heyday Books.

Kevles, B. (1997) *Naked to the bone: Medical imaging in the twentieth century*, New Brunswick: Rutgers University Press.

Kmietowicz, Z. (2005) 'NHS criticised for lax control', *British Medical Journal*, vol 330, no 805 (9 April), doi:10.1136/bmj.330.7495.805.

Marx, K. (1954 [1867]) *Capital: Volume 1: A critique of political economy*, London: Lawrence and Wishart.

Marx, K. and Engels, F. (1998 [1848]) *The communist manifesto*, London: Penguin Books.

McKeown T. (1976) *The role of medicine: Dream, mirage, or nemesis?* London: Nuffield Provincial Hospitals Trust.

McQuaig, L. (2005) *The need to relate to other humans*, Rabble (www.rabble.ca/columnists/need–relate-other-humans).

Navarro, V. (1976) *Medicine under capitalism*, New York: Prodist.

Navarro, V. (1978) *Class struggle, the state and medicine: An historical and contemporary analysis of the medical sector in Great Britain*, London: Martin Robertson.

Navarro, V. (1986) *Crisis, health and medicine*, London: Tavistock Publications.

Null, G. et al (2003) *Death by medicine, Part I* (www.healthelivingnews.com/articles/death_by_medicine_prt_1.html).

OECD (Organisation for Economic Cooperation and Development) (2003) *Health data*, Paris: OECD, Table 10 (www.oecd.org/dataoecd/1/31/2957323.x1s).

Parsons, T. (1964 [1951]) *The social system*, New York: Free Press.

Polanyi, K. (1957 [1944]) *The great transformation: The political and economic origins of our time*, Boston: Beacon Press by arrangement with Rinehart & Company Inc.

Porter, R. (1999) *The greatest benefit to mankind: A medical history of humanity*, New York: Norton.

Russell, L.B. (1979) *Technology in hospitals: Medical advances and their diffusion*, Washington, DC: Brookings Institution.

Sargent, M. (2003) *Citizenship and the Medical Sciences,* National Institute for Medical Research (www.nimr.mrc.ac.uk/millhillessays/2003/citizen/).

Sayer, A. (2003) 'Developing the critical standpoints of radical political economy', Paper presented at 'Marxism today: A renewed left view', Havana, Cuba, 17–19 February 2000 (www.lancs.ac.uk/fass/sociology/papers/sayer-critical-standpoints-of-radical-political-economy.pdf).

Socialist Health Association (2005) *The pharmaceutical industry* (www.sochealth.co.uk).

Sunday Times (1999) 'Blunders by doctors kill 40,000 per year', 19 December.

Watkins, C. et al (2003) 'Characteristics of general practitioners who frequently see drug industry representatives: national cross sectional study', *British Medical Journal*, vol 326, pp 1178-9.

Wright, E.O. (1978) *Class, crisis and the state*, London: Verso.

Zola, I. (1972) 'Medicine as an institution of social control', *Sociological Review*, vol 4, pp 487–504.

THREE

Orthodox, complementary and alternative medicines

Ultimately the power of the medical profession still appears to be the stumbling block to ending the marginalisation of alternative therapists in Britain in the future, despite the growth in consumer interest in seeking assistance from such practitioners. (Saks, 1994, p 93)

Complementary and alternative medicine (CAM) has become a popular form of healthcare and the predictions are that it will increase further. The reasons for this level of popularity are highly diverse, and much of the motivation to turn to CAM pertains to a deeply felt criticism of mainstream medicine. (Aston, 2001, p 90)

Introduction

In this chapter we engage with the concept of 'late modernity' (or 'high modernity') as a broader theme for producing an understanding of medicalisation. The previous chapter ended with the claim that the Marxist approach may offer more scope than Illich's critique of medicine for producing knowledge of how medical practice and its consequences are mediated by the definitions of health and illness inscribed within the capitalist economy. The latter are based on the requirements for functionally productive labour, as well as by the requirement that use values and social needs, such as those for healthcare, either enhance or, at worst, do not set insurmountable limits to the requirements of the capitalist economy for profit.

This chapter examines medicalisation from within a different conceptual framework that ultimately differs from Marxism, that of late modernity. While the concept of late modernity will be developed at length below, briefly it refers to the idea that science and professional institutions have the last word on truth when it is brought into doubt. The belief in hidden laws of nature and society is rejected, along with claims related to this, concerning universally applicable principles of justice. Moreover, a greater emphasis is placed on differences between individuals and on the choices and opportunities available. Identities, which before were seen as fixed and shaped in terms of class structure, are now recognised as more fluid and uncertain. Individuals are more likely to view themselves in terms of shifting identities, including those of gender, ethnicity and class. Moreover, identities are increasingly expressed through consumption, not work. Hence they are likely to be more transient and more individualised.

In summary, late modernity is shorthand for the shift away from the traditional structures through which we live out our lives – such as social class position, taken-for-granted assumptions regarding gender, and old certainties such as the tendency to see science as inherently progressive. These perceived certainties arose in modern industrial society, only to become normalised as essential enduring truths. In this sense, late modernity is understood as the completion of modernity's failure to reflect critically on its own foundations and false certainties, which had come to act as a break on human emancipation (for example, the false certainty of putting too much faith in scientific knowledge systems; foundations that naturalised social class differences and gender divisions, and so on) (Williams and Calnan, 1996; Lash, 1999; Heaphy, 2007).

In this chapter we will discuss two competing perspectives on late modernity, one associated with Giddens (1991), the other with Habermas (1987). One could argue that each perspective represents either side of the contradiction referred to by Marxists, between the potential for medicine to take a commodified route or to become increasingly decommodified; the former being more conducive to the medicalisation of society, the latter having tendencies towards demedicalisation. As a context for assessing the contribution of the concept of late modernity to understanding the contradictory trends within medicalisation, the chapter will focus on the growing popularity of complementary and alternative medicine (CAM) and implications that follow from this popularity for the status and continuing authority of orthodox medicine. However, before we engage fully with the concept of late modernity, the chapter first provides a brief introductory commentary on how CAM is defined and its recent growth in popularity.

CAM: a brief overview

CAM is not easy to define. Partly this is because different cultures have different ideas about what is orthodox – and so, also, about what is alternative (Fennell et al, 2009, p 72). In Western societies 'alternative' medicines tend to be defined simply as medicines preferred in place of biomedicine, while 'complementary' medicine tends to be medicine that is more easily integrated with biomedicine as a range of treatments. CAM is thus a shorthand umbrella term. CAM is also variously known as 'non-traditional medicine', 'unorthodox medical practices', and 'holistic healthcare'. Moreover, the difficulty in defining CAM is due to the fact that it stands for a diverse range of medicines which target different aspects of the person. Some CAMs, for example, focus on the vitalism of the body, through the administration of herbs, food, vitamins and diet. Other CAMs focus on the mind, through relaxation techniques, art, dance, and so on. Others still focus on energy fields, through various touch therapies such as Reiki. Finally, other CAMs focus on the physical manipulation of the body through massage, chiropractic, and so on (NCCAM, 2009).

The 'first ever comprehensive Inquiry into Complementary and Alternative Medicine (CAM) in the UK by a Parliamentary Select Committee' divided CAM, on a sliding scale of health risk and professionalism, into 'principle disciplines' regulated by Acts of Parliament and supported by recognised diagnostics, such as chiropractics and acupuncture; non-diagnostic complementaries to conventional medicine, including aromatherapy and reflexology; and 'other disciplines' that 'purport' to have diagnostic skills but which are of different philosophical origin from those of conventional medicine, including ayurvedic and traditional Chinese medicines (Department of Health, 2001).

However one defines CAM, the upsurge of interest in alternative medicines in developed countries is not in dispute. Today acupuncture, osteopathy and homeopathy are almost mainstream medicine, while there has been a dramatic rise in interest in treatments such as reflexology, massage, Reiki and aromatherapy (Bodeker and Kronenberg, 2002, p 1582). Various estimates suggest that, towards the end of the 1990s, the percentage of populations that had used one form of CAM or another was on an upward spiral; for example, one estimate indicated '46% in Australia, 49% in France and 70% in Canada' and one in five of the population in Britain (Ernst, 2000). Up to 22 million visits were made to CAM practitioners of acupuncture, chiropractic, homeopathy, herbalism and osteopathy (Ernst, 2000). NHS hospitals in England also had 14 million visits and up to half of all GPs had offered alternative medicine to their patients in 2001 (Thomas, 2008, p 360). The World Health Organization described how:

> In the US, total 1997 out-of-pocket CAM expenditure was estimated at US$ 2700 million, which was comparable to the projected 1997 out-of-pocket expenditure for all physician services.... In the United Kingdom, annual CAM expenditure is estimated at US$ 2300 million respectively.... In Canada, it is estimated that a total of US$ 2400 million was spent in 1997 on CAM. (WHO, 2002)

Over-the-counter use of CAM has also become increasingly popular. Mintel International Group (2005) suggests that, for the UK, 'the consumer market for alternative medicine and its products has grown by 45% in real terms from 1999 to 2004. Most market growth has come from herbal and homeopathic remedies, with essential oils not quite keeping pace. Sales of herbal medicines account for more than half of category value, having risen by 16% since 2002, while homeopathic remedies have experienced a 10% rise in value over the same period, and sales of aromatherapy essential oils have increased by 8%.'

Current estimates indicate there are up to 50,000 CAM practitioners in the UK and that one in four of the population are CAM users, in an industry worth £1.6 billion (Newton et al, 2008). According to Fulder (1996, p 105), the 'radical renewal of interest' is so significant that 'conventional medicine sees itself actually threatened by an unscientific rival. Many are now visualising a future for western medicine in which it shares and competes for customers with alternative medicine, within a pluralistic medical system.'This re-evaluation is reflected in the changing attitude of the British Medical Association (BMA) to CAM in recent years (BMA, 1992; 1993). The *British Medical Journal* (2001) has reflected on the apparent sea-change in attitudes towards CAM in two major reports undertaken by the BMA, the first in 1986 and the second in 1993. While the first report was still very critical towards CAM, the 1993 report, although recording its differences, was more sanguine and there was a definite shift towards viewing alternatives as 'complementary'. This sea-change was also evidenced by the increased willingness among GPs to offer some forms of alternative medicine. The *British Medical Journal* (2001, p 119) estimated that by 2001 around 39.5% of general practice partnerships in England provided access to some form of complementary therapy for their NHS patients, and was able to report 'a major increase in orthodox medicine courses familiarising students with complementary and alternative medicine'.

The above picture does indicate that a radical change in perspective of some form is under way with regard to many people's approaches to health and medicine. One has to bear in mind that, prior to this resurgence of interest in CAM, biomedicine had no rivals of any substance since it came to ascendancy in the UK after the 1858 Medical Registration Act. The General Medical Council established by this Act gave notice at that time, and for more than 100 years thereafter, as to who could and could not be included on its Register as a provider of legitimate medical practice to the public at large (Roberts, 2009). Indeed, once established, the dominance of biomedicine became consolidated with the development of the welfare state in the early part of the 20th century. In particular, the 1911 National Insurance Act saw the state take a more direct hand in using the public purse to pay for biomedicine-oriented healthcare, and this served to further marginalise alternative medical practices – the state paid only for 'legitimate' medicine, not for 'chicanery' (Lawrence, 1994; Porter, 1997). The emergence of the post-1945 welfare state and of the NHS saw the completion of biomedicine's claim to be the official form of medicine. In this sense, 'alternative' forms of medicine acquired greater meaning for their name, by becoming well and truly cast out to the margins of society. As Saks (1994, p 87) observes, 'the term alternative medicine refers not so much to the content of these therapies – which are marked by considerable heterogeneity – as to their predominant outsider status within the British health care system'.

Notwithstanding this brief historical recap, the question remains: how are we to understand the present-day growth in popularity of CAM? What significance does the rise in the demand for alternative forms of medicine and healthcare have for orthodox medicine? If biomedical dominance is given meaning by the marginalisation of alternative forms of medical practice, then perhaps the more crucial question is to what extent the growing popularity of CAM represents a serious challenge to medical orthodoxy and the seemingly ongoing march of medicalisation.

In what follows, we assess the very different interpretations of the concept of late modernity offered by Giddens and Habermas as a means of illuminating the broader social reasons for the growth in popularity of CAM. In particular, we will focus on the following three claims: (1) that the popularity of CAM is related to disenchantment with orthodox medicine under the conditions of post-industrial society; (2) that the growing use of CAM is a by-product of orthodox medicine's desire to incorporate complementary medicines within its empire; and (3) that this latter strategic incorporation of CAM into orthodox medicine is fundamental to health policy.

With the above objectives in mind, the remainder of the chapter will explore the following claims:

- that the growing popularity of CAM has been driven by a pervasive disenchantment on the part of the public with its experiences of orthodox medicine;
- that this disenchantment is facilitated and underpinned by broader transformations, including what Giddens describes as the shift from traditional modern society to late modernity;
- that Habermas's concepts of 'systems world' and 'life world' can help to provide a theoretical framework for a more nuanced understanding of the relationship between CAM and orthodoxy as one of struggle, which is part rapprochement and part repulsion;
- that rather than challenge alternative medicine, the increased adaption to CAM is part of biomedicine's incorporation of CAM into a more broadly defined orthodoxy;
- that this incorporation is aided by the legitimating authority of the state in search of cost-containment strategies within a policy framework that is influenced by discourses of consumer choice.

Giddens, high modernity and the growing popularity of CAM

How is the growing popularity of CAM to be explained? Sociologists point to a number of key changes to social class structures, patterns of employment and family relations over the last three decades, which are gathered as evidence of late (or high) modernity and which may help in understanding the rising popularity of CAM.

Giddens (1991) argues that we are in the thrall of high modernity, characterised by the breakdown in traditional norms, values and beliefs that underpinned trust in institutions, and where an increasingly reflexive and critical citizenship places institutions and expert knowledge systems under scrutiny. Social relations and links between people are becoming increasingly stretched, across both local and global frontiers, with the arrival of the internet and satellite media; social divisions based on class, gender and race are weakening; and individuals are relatively more dispersed and socially mobile.

Individuals in *traditional society* have a more familiar sense of place and know their social roles; they live in traditional family structures, such as the nuclear family, where fathers, mothers, brothers and sisters know the roles they perform.

And this traditional family is supported and sustained by a welfare state based on the principle of the male breadwinner. Consumption and production follow standard patterns, with mass-produced, standardised housing, means of transport, food and clothing and so on. Leisure is similarly standardised and has definite class patterns. Employment is full time and is patterned along white- and blue-collar class lines, and unemployment and job uncertainty remain marginal. In other words, life is very ordered, with a great deal of certainty about how one's own personal biography will be lived out.

By comparison, individuals in *high modernity* experience something very different. The concept of high modernity refers to recent trends, whereby social relations are less fixed, more chaotic and uncertain. There has been a marked increase in rates of divorce since the 1960s. Family roles have changed too, with a variety of family structures, including lone-parent families, families with two parents previously married to other partners, families with and without blood-related children, and so on. Social life is increasingly more secular in the West, which means that we no longer tend to understand our place in the world as given by God or derive our values from religious belief systems. Employment has shifted from the male-breadwinner model to one in which there are increasingly more women in employment, who see it as a defining characteristic of their identity. Related to this, more job opportunities are now opening up to women vis-à-vis men; and the mass redundancies and job losses of the 1980s and 1990s were of male full-time jobs. This latter fact signifies a profound change in the status and identities of men and of women. Finally, for both middle and working classes, work itself has changed; working hours are no longer 9 till 5, and working contracts no longer guarantee a career structure but are increasingly fixed, temporary or part time.

Moreover, Giddens views the transformation in employment, religious beliefs and family–work relationships on the one hand as posing a very real threat to the economic, moral and social security of people, but on the other hand as simultaneously acting as a possible catalyst for 'fresh opportunities' and 'emotional growth'. Individuals, once freed from traditional securities and social constraints, are exposed to considerable life risks, yet this freedom also means that they now have the potential to change their biographies. In traditional society our lives are lived as if someone else has written the script and we live out the roles provided for us. In contrast, high modernity offers us the potential to write our own 'story'. Indeed, the increased responsibility to find employment in an uncertain job market and the greater choice over family lifestyles also imply that in high modernity we are invested with a greater sense of *individualism*, which inspires an enhanced capacity to reflect on ourselves and on our own social and personal predicaments. We develop, in other words, a greater sense of *reflexivity*: that is, we all become much more aware that our lives can be transformed by our own actions; more aware of our own role and the role that others can play in reshaping our social worlds. We no longer *have* a biography, we *live* our biography.

Giddens situates the rising popularity of alternative forms of medicine within the overall shift towards high modernity. The changes inherent in high modernity are *ambiguous* for those involved, because they offer both potential opportunities and possible sources of stress and exploitation. In this respect, high modernity produces a conceptual framework which represents medicalisation as being in tension with a demedicalising agenda. In this view, the 'bottom-up challenge' to orthodox medicine posed by the growing demand for complementary and alternative medicines is emblematic of a more reflexive society in which individuals and collective movements have greater access to medical information flows, are more critically aware of the limits to orthodoxy and are more open to the possibilities of alternatives. Within Giddens' conceptual understanding of high modernity, reflexive individuals rely less on the traditional authority embedded in Parsons' concept of doctor–patient relations. They are more reliant on their rights and responsibilities as citizens for their own health promotion, and are generally more confident about their own lay knowledge. The latter does not allay doubt and uncertainty; indeed doubt permeates all aspects of health and medicine, as individuals grapple with contesting 'systems of accumulated expertise ... representing multiple sources of authority' (Giddens, 1991, p 3) that become pivotal to our biographies. 'The upshot' is that:

> all beliefs and practices are subject to systematic examination, critical scrutiny and revision in the light of changing social circumstances. Reflexivity, therefore, becomes a chronic and defining feature of 'late' modernity, involving a never ending cycle of re-appraisals, re-assessments and revisions which span all aspects of modern social life. (Williams and Calnan, 1996, p 1612)

This broader context symbolises and facilitates the emergence of new social movements – environmental, feminist, New Age, and so on – which offer new insights to individuals to re-enchant their social world through reflexive critical practices and ideas based on meanings and values that offer a source of counter-vailing power to the authority of medicine.

The disenchantment with orthodox medicine

Giddens' particular interpretation of high modernity enables the turn towards alternative medicines to be represented as part of an emerging movement to engage with health-related knowledge flows that enable the lay public to wrest back some control of the medicalisation agenda (Cant and Sharma, 1998, p 25). This is facilitated by that greater sense of risk that prevails once one realises that medical expertise may be found wanting and cannot be trusted per se, but must be interrogated: trust must be earned and medicine must learn to accept the relevance of lay and alternative voices, while the latter must live with an environment in which knowledge is mediated through various media and competing interests (Williams and Calnan, 1996).

It is suggested that individuals, driven by disenchantment, are deconstructing the boundaries between lay knowledge and expert knowledge (Prior, 2003). In particular, while medical knowledge and practice has always been culturally mediated and reinterpreted, the spread and breadth of information about chronic health issues among the lay public provides a context for people to become intimately aware of the experience of illness and what works best for them, all of which provides fertile ground for experimentation and acceptance of complementary and alternative forms of medicine (Cant and Sharma, 1998, pp 22–3). As a result, the belief that 'the doctor knows best' is increasingly being challenged by people looking for something different than orthodox medicine. People are looking to be treated as people, instead of as carriers of a disease; looking to become part of their own cure and to take an active part in their own illness prevention and health promotion. In sum, alternative medicine is becoming popular because of a general and pervasive disenchantment with biomedicine. The trend towards an increase in chronic and long-term forms of ill-health is leading to people potentially becoming lay experts in their own treatments, drawing on years of experience and the kinds of intuition that are inaccessible to doctors (Gabe et al, 1994).

Moreover, where biomedicine tends to treat people as 'bundles of cells' and body parts (Cant and Sharma, 1998, p 24), alternative medicine offers bedside medicine for the modern era, in which the person's beliefs, emotions and feelings are central to the medical encounter. As this alternative experience develops, biomedicine's epistemic power to 'know the body' is increasingly challenged by a more reflexive and informed public, aided by the greater dissemination of medical knowledge through the internet (Eysenbach et al, 1999, p 1). This greater awareness and critical reflective attitude to medicine has, in turn, furthered people's propensity to seek out alternative forms of medicine that prioritise what they are looking for in terms of health needs, advice and treatment; an approach specific to needs, which perhaps is not entirely shaped around the quick fix or cure (Cant and Sharma, 1998).

As explained in the preceding chapter, disenchantment with orthodox medicine also arises in the context of the medical-driven scandals surrounding the misuse of drugs, drug side effects and the mounting catalogue of medical errors in which medicine appears to be increasingly involved, which only serves to heighten the public's sense of distrust in medicine (Velanovich et al, 2006, p 210) – a distrust which gains even more momentum with disclosures about the propensity of medicine to close professional ranks in order to protect its own interests, rather than the public good. Complaints and malpractice litigation against the medical profession are a rising trend in the UK (Allsop, 2006, p 626). Media scandals concerning the infringement of patient rights as a result of poor medical recording, lax handling of complaints, and the gender bias of a male-dominated profession that is experienced by women when the profession fails to prioritise everyday health problems of women, give added impetus to the turn away from orthodox medicine and towards alternative medicine (Oakley, 1993).

Some also suggest that, as a consequence of this disenchantment, lay knowledge of health and illness is acquiring greater priority in contemporary society (Williams and Popay, 1994). People approach health and illness in a more holistic way, which draws on references from their own experience over matters of the onset and development of illness. Increasingly, the 'lay expert' within us desires more than knowledge of 'what caused my condition', to include 'what is the cause and what meaning does it have to me and the direction of my life'. Questions that are, perhaps, vital to individuals, but that medicine is not capable of addressing, are: 'Why is it happening to me? And why is it happening now?' Accordingly, the more holistic and interpretive framework of alternative medicines, which does claim to prioritise subjectivity, appears to be more in keeping with lay knowledge and expectations.

Indeed, Kleinman and Seeman (2000) refer to people's growing discontent with the way in which orthodox medicine ignores the cultural and moral experiences surrounding illness and its meaning for individuals. Those whose lives are most touched by illness – the ill person and relatives and friends – can often resist the classifications imposed on the illness by medicine and embrace definitions intimately expressing the cultural patterns and personal experiences of sickness which are fundamental to healing but which are often excluded from the treatment offered by orthodox medicine. For example, heart disease may be to do with faulty valves and thickening arteries, but it is also just as much to do with the patient's *lived experience* of having a weak heart and how this affects the person's identity and their intimate relations with others. As the authors put it, 'we need also to take account of an illness's "powerful destructive ripple effect on the life world" of the person and their kith and kin' (Kleinman and Seeman, 2000, p 201).

As a result, disaffection with orthodox medicine, and the related attraction of alternative medicines, may be explained by biomedical orthodoxy's ignorance of key *illness narratives*. In this respect, Frank (2000) draws attention to four key illness narratives that individuals may draw upon at any one time to give meaning and understanding to their situations. Frank refers to the *restitution narrative*, concerning how one copes with illness; the *chaos narrative*, concerning feelings of fear and anger surrounding the loss of someone or some function; *quest narratives*, emphasising the search for cure; and *testimony narratives*, reflecting on what has been lost and gained from the experience of illness. All the narratives have a bearing on the way illness and the patient are treated, but the time and financial constraints on orthodox medicine, as it is currently organised, mean that the resources and time to develop them are missing.

In summary, the above narrative is a product of conceptual readings of late modernity and of the opportunities this conceptual reading provides for challenging orthodoxy, as put forward by Giddens. It is interesting, in this respect, to recall for a moment the contradiction, outlined in the previous chapter, between the commodification of medicine, which highlights its instrumental nature, on the one hand, and the struggle to assert the development of what is useful and specific about medicine to the needs of social groups, on the other hand. Viewed through this conceptual prism, it is as if Giddens tends to emphasise the latter part of the contradiction (development of a person-focused medicine) in his optimistic reading of late modernity, at the expense of, perhaps naively, downgrading the still powerful forces of commodification and instrumentality with respect to late modernity in general and its application to medicine in particular. However, it has been argued that critical reflexivity may not be as pervasive as the above arguments suggest. For one thing, not all social groups have the money or opportunity to take up CAM and to make tangible their reservations about orthodox medicine. Research by Cant and Sharma (1998) revealed that users of alternative and complementary medicines are predominantly middle-class women. Thomas and Coleman (2004, p 152), in their survey, note 'a significant positive association between CAM use and non-manual social class', level of full-time education and earning power over £15,600 per annum. The data indicate that those who are socially and economically disadvantaged may have less access to critical information flows, are more inclined to be dependent on GPs and are therefore excluded from those 'reflexive actors who are willing and able to challenge the dominant expert authority' of medicine (Ward, 2007, p 130). Moreover, attitudes towards medicine are highly variable, depending on local circumstance, for example, the quality of one's GP and local health authority, and so on, and while some GPs and hospital environments prove to be alienating, others may be much more humane (Ward, 2007, p 127). The more notice we give such data, the more questionable these broad-sweeping, optimistic notions of reflexive social movements challenging the power of medicine become.

These criticisms do not rule out disenchantment in the context of 'reflexive modernity' as a driving force in the popularity of CAM. They do, however, question its primacy and, therefore, lead one to reflect that, while disenchantment with orthodox medicine may provide a reasonable explanation for the greater popularity of CAM, other factors must also be involved. Indeed, as the chapter now goes on to highlight, the emergence of CAM may be more nuanced and limited in its challenge to orthodox medicine and the medicalisation of society – as a result of what Habermas describes as the continuing tensions between *system* and *life worlds*, which, he argues, remain as pervasive in late modernity as they did in modern or traditional society. As we also go on to demonstrate, this more pessimistic conceptual reading of late modernity dovetails with Weber's critique of professional power.

The power of orthodox medicine to incorporate alternatives

So far it has been suggested that the growing popularity of alternative and complementary medicine is being driven from below by a more reflexive populace, increasingly disenchanted with orthodox medicine and within the more supportive environment of late modernity, as understood by Giddens. However, late modernity is still related to modernity; the power of professional institutions may be attenuated but they still remain intact. In this respect, perhaps it is also the case that the continued challenge 'from above' (from medical orthodoxy) is equally relevant to consider. In what follows we consider orthodox medicine's ability to incorporate alternative medicine, and in the process to dilute the radical potential of the latter while boosting the influence that orthodox medicine wields within society.

It is useful at this point to consider Habermas's account of the irresistible qualities of the 'systems world' vis-à-vis the 'life world'. Habermas (1971) refers to the 'systems world' as those areas of society where larger structures of predefined rules dominate individuals and treat people as a means to an end – through which people tend to uncritically accept as 'second nature' the prevailing structures and rules governing the economy (money, science, bureaucratic organisation, and so on). We get a sense of what Habermas is driving at by referring back to the Marxist critique of medicine as a commodity and Illich's observations that people are cogs in the machine of 'industrial society', which we discussed in Chapter Two. Habermas argues that the 'systems world' is liable to 'colonise' (encroach upon and subordinate) the 'life world' – the countervailing rich source of intersubjective meaning, local customs, community involvement, social solidarity and discursive rather than abstract knowledge.

The 'life world' refers to ideas and practices that are communicated through culture and mediated through myths, symbols and rituals, a world of intersubjective understanding and communication between people treated as ends in themselves rather than means to an end (that is, people treated instrumentally). 'At the level of the life world we aim to make sense of social processes as the outcome of social actors' intentions and value orientations' (Goode, 2005, p 63). The systems world refers to the social structures humans create, such as bureaucratic institutions, the economy, markets, and so on, which gain a life of their own and constrain human agency and life world ideas and practices to the imperatives of efficiency, organisation and technical control. Under modernity, the systems world goes largely unchecked in its dominance over the life world, and to this degree the project of modernity remains unfinished.

Late modernity signifies the intensification of this struggle between life world and systems world. Habermas (1978) suggests that inherent in human communication is the need to build consensus and progress society. His conceptual narrative of late modernity is that it signifies an era with the potential for developing human communication across the boundaries of life and systems worlds, and thus has the potential for creating a more sustainable balance or fusion between life and system world imperatives. Both imperatives are driven by enduring human interests, and so are permanent features of society; prior to late modernity, however, system world interests dominated, to the detriment of life world. When the interest is to produce wealth and advance technological progress through, say, the economy and the division of labour and so on, then the overriding societal interest gravitates decisively towards efficiency and calculability. In short, we have an interest in developing technical knowledge and using technical (instrumental) language to describe human interactions and interests. Priority is given to the logical exposition of efficiency of means to achieve ends, whether the end is making money, producing products or human communication. However, what never becomes obscured is that we also have other interests, and so, other approaches to knowledge that cater to these interests. Firstly, we have an interest in understanding and empathising with others and developing a grasp of shared meanings and so on. In other words, we have an interest in developing hermeneutic knowledge about our place in culture and within systems of shared meaning. Secondly, we have an in-built interest in emancipatory knowledge, which is knowledge aimed at critical reflection on what is right and wrong, moral or unethical: what is the good life. The latter are what Giddens prioritises. Habermas's point is that we also need to prioritise how the systems world interrelates with the latter, because it is not going to disappear and, if left unmanaged, has dominated and will continue to dominate all aspects of life, including the interrelationship between medicine and society.

For Habermas, both 'worlds' are fundamental to social progress and human interests. Hence, his approach to the concept of late modernity is defined by the hope for a more progressive fusion between system and life worlds (the unfinished business of modernity), but also by the recognition that this is not pre-ordained, there is always the possibility of systemic dominance, and colonisation remains a reality. Of course we inhabit one world; Habermas's point, though, is that our world is in tension/struggle to articulate life and system world values.

What implications for medicine and an understanding of the significance of CAM flow from Habermas's conceptual approach to late modernity? One implication emerges if we position medical science as part of the systems world, reducing people to calculable body parts to be 're-engineered' by experts; and if we position alternative and complementary medical practices as part of the life world on the basis that the life world emphasises the whole person and places priority on negotiated healthcare. Another implication follows from highlighting the tension between the systems world and the life world, which can often be a struggle between one and the other. The two implications suggest that, while Habermas recognises the potential for a more reflexive society as a basis for the emergence of CAM, late modernity also provides fertile ground for re-establishing the dominating influence of 'systems world' imperatives driving orthodox medicine. We see this tension in the tendency for homeopathy to flourish, only for the terms of its legitimacy to be then drawn back within 'evidence-based medical practice', which has its basis in medical science. Hence, in 'late modern' 'reflexive society' there remains the very real potential to corrupt new social movements and rein back/subvert what is novel or enchanted in medical practice through their reintegration into the 'systems world'. However, the opposite is also possible: alternative practices and ideas in the 'life world' could shake off existing constraints that threaten to colonise and so erode their intrinsic meaning, and perhaps even invest 'systems world medicine' (biomedicine) with new meaning and a greater sense of humanism.

Habermas helps us to pose the question left largely unexplored by competing versions of late modernity: to what extent is greater power exerted by orthodox medicine to restrain CAM within the systems world, in such as way that it erodes its life world–affirming potential? Adopting Habermas's conceptual understanding of late modernity, it could be argued that the growing demand for alternative forms of medicine is due to its being incorporated by orthodox medicine – as a means of defence against those alternatives deemed to represent a growing threat to its continued legitimacy. Weber (1978) argued that as well as the more benign characteristics associated with 'professions', such as duty of service, maintenance of standards of practice and training, and so on, there exists a set of power dynamics that come to the fore whenever the profession is perceived to be under threat. Threats may come from other occupational groups in close proximity who strive to achieve professional status in orthodox medicine's field of expertise (the nursing profession is one example, but so too are alternative medical practitioners). Equally, the threat can arise when the status of orthodox professional practice and knowledge base is brought into question by the public. As we have noted, orthodox medicine is experiencing both of these. Weber (1978) argued that when professional groups feel threatened, then the profession does one of two things: either it closes its ranks and exerts political power to maintain its ascendancy through, for example, pressure group activity to maintain legitimacy, or it begins to think about broadening out its knowledge base by *incorporating other expert knowledge systems into its own*, thus reconstituting its authority in the eyes of the public while displacing the perceived threat (through incorporating aspects of its knowledge base).

To what extent does the incorporation of alternative medicines by biomedicine represent another reason for its growing popularity? Moreover, to what extent does the flip side of this growing popularity signify the medicalisation of alternative medicines?

Saks (1994, p 85) highlights the nature of the potential threat that CAM poses to orthodoxy in the following way:

> The popular support of alternative medicine has posed a potential threat to the biomedical principles under-pinning the activities and professional standing of medical orthodoxy, in which the body tends to be viewed as a machine whose parts can be repaired on breakdown. This threat is centrally embodied in the characteristically more holistic approach of alternative practitioners operating largely outside the orthodox profession who show a greater degree of recognition of the importance of the relationship between mind and body in individual diagnosis and treatment.

Having initially ousted alternative medicine following the introduction of the 1858 Medical Registration Act and subsequent 1911 National Health Insurance Act and 1946 NHS Act, orthodox medicine would now appear to be tackling the perceived threat from CAM by reversing its hostility and seeking to bring alternatives back into the mainstream (Saks, 1994). We can see this occurring in a limited way. For example, and as noted earlier, over the last three decades there has been a growth in the use of acupuncture by GPs and an increasing recognition of the role of massage and reflexology. Moreover, chiropractic procedures have become recognised by both medical orthodoxy and the state as a medical procedure for dealing with back ailments. Thus, typical of incorporation, the growing legitimacy of alternative medicine is limited and often redefined in terms more favourable to orthodoxy. So, for example, acupuncture is accepted, but its wider origins in Yin–Yang theories of mind–body relations are not. Chiropractic is recognised, but only insofar as its more radical holistic understandings of the body are jettisoned for those of biomedicine.

The above examples bring to light two sides of incorporation: the first is to disarm the threat from alternatives by aligning their traditional knowledge base and regulatory framework within a biomedicine frame of reference. Hence, *medicalisation* becomes the mechanism for disarming the perceived threat to orthodoxy that is posed by alternative medicine. For example, the World Health Organization (WHO, 2002) has urged the use of biomedical benchmarks such as evidenced-based practice and rational rules-based legitimacy to judge the validity of alternative medicines before they can be included within the mainstream. The second side is to extend the authority of orthodox medicine by directly engaging in and effecting control over these new areas of practice. So, for example, in a recent study of interaction between biomedical and alternative practitioners in an organised setting, Hollenberg (2006, p 731) wrote that 'findings from a research study of two newly established Integrated Health Care (IHC) settings in Canada … revealed that biomedical practitioners enact patterns of exclusionary and demarcationary closure, in addition to the use of "esoteric knowledge", by: (a) dominating patient charting, referrals and diagnostic tests; (b) regulating CAM practitioners to a specific "sphere of competence"; (c) appropriating certain CAM techniques from less powerful CAM professions; and (d) using biomedical language as the primary mode of communication. CAM practitioners, in turn, perform their own closure strategies.'

Incorporation of one sort or another has been a fundamental part of the growth and development of orthodox medicine as we know it today. Incorporation has been an effective means through which medicine's expanding social influence has been maintained. Armstrong (2002) notes the spread of medical surveillance over the population over two centuries, from bedside medicine, to hospital and clinically based medicine. Medicine has incorporated itself with various dispositions towards the body and populations, and in doing so has shifted its areas of control and surveillance over a population's health and illness. In this context, the current extension of orthodoxy into alternative practices may be understood as part of a wider shift in the surveillance of medicine, of perhaps more recent origin, from the clinic into the community. In particular, the signs and symptoms of the unhealthy body have now been extended to the community, where signs and symptoms are now conjoined with 'risks' of becoming ill. As Armstrong expands (2002):

> The blurring of the distinction between health and illness, between the normal and the pathological, meant that healthcare intervention could no longer focus almost exclusively on the body of the patient in the hospital bed. Medical surveillance would have to leave the hospital and penetrate into the wider population.

Perhaps one implication we could draw from this is that the incorporation of alternative medicine by orthodox medicine assists and facilitates the extension of orthodox medicine's influence beyond the clinic and into the community, and especially to a reflexive public eager for medical information. Perversely, the preoccupation with CAM may be both a result of counter-cultural resistance to orthodoxy or pragmatism on the part of health consumers and also another means through which society becomes increasingly medically conscious or medicalised. Knowledge flows that generate information about CAM are assimilated to mechanical metaphors of the body that potentially expose the body to more extensive systems of medical and health surveillance (Fadlon, 2004). If we accept this proposition for the moment, the question arises to what extent can orthodox medicine act alone in this incorporation/medicalisation of alternative medicines? To what extent are other interests also embroiled in the incorporation of alternative medicine into the mainstream? As Friedson (1988) argued, medicalisation is driven by a combination of medical, economic and political interests. Below, we consider the role of the state.

The state and alternative medicine

As outlined above, incorporation within the domain of orthodox medicine may be one major factor in explaining the wider usage of alternative medicine. However, Cant and Sharma (2002) also point out that the more favourable climate that alternative medicines such as chiropractic and osteopathy enjoy is also due to the influence of the state in medical matters.

The state has also played a part in encouraging this *incorporation*, for its own end and as a means of promoting 'consumer choice' and managing the spiralling costs of healthcare (Cant and Sharma, 2002). Extending the legitimacy to practise medicine to a selection of alternative medicines enables the state to increase the supply of medical professionals to the community, and at a relatively lower cost in terms of treatment, as compared with the costs associated with training orthodox medical professionals. Successive UK governments have sought to extend the role and function of medicine within a community setting; the introduction of alternatives also helps to sustain this policy, and supports the emphasis increasingly placed on health promotion programmes. This dovetails with the related government encouragement of private healthcare provision and the development of a market for healthcare which positions patients as consumers, and health and medical care as products within the context of a consumer-driven society.

There have been a number of specific state responses over the previous three decades aimed at the incorporation of certain types of alternative medicines. For example, 1987 saw the introduction of the Osteopathy and Chiropractors Act. Here, the state gave professional legitimacy to these two alternative medical practices, in return for their agreement to establish core professional norms and training practices, *overseen by orthodox medicine*. The 1990 NHS and Community Care Act also set in motion a fundamental reform of the NHS, by introducing market competition between hospitals and between GPs. A key component of this reform was to decentralise to GP fundholders the decision making over which packages of care they purchased from suppliers. The Conservative government specifically stated that fund-holder GPs should consider all forms of medical and healthcare packages, including alternatives. The same 1990 NHS and Community Care Act also saw the development of the Family Health Service Authority, which could act independently as provider or purchaser of primary and social care, and which has increasingly drawn on a range of alternative healthcare and medical arrangements for families and individuals. This role was later given increased emphasis when the Labour government, post-1997, created primary care units within a rearranged NHS that were given a determining role in commissioning healthcare and medicine. The refocus on primary and social care has also moved health closer to the market, and a language of consumerism is now as extensive as the range of alternative medicines that one can demand.

These incorporation tendencies run parallel with the tendency for the state to attempt to bring alternative medicines within a unified regulatory framework. In this respect, the Foundation of Integrated Medicine, the Centre for Complementary Health Studies (CCHS) and the House of Lords (2002) have been the main health and government institutions for achieving consensus over the regulation of CAM. However, given the plurality of alternative and complementary medicines, the state is caught between attempting to impose statutory regulation, on the one hand, and drawing back from this to encourage CAMs to self-regulate, on the other hand. The immediate motive for formal regulation is perhaps the safety of patients. However, the overall approach adopted by the state towards regulation does more to ensure that the professionalisation of very different forms of medicines occurs within an over-arching discourse with respect to standards that are based on abstracted codes of professional conduct and continuing professional development. Alternative practitioners, faced with having to devise professional self-regulatory practices for the first time, will naturally draw on what is already available, which is to say the language and discourse of statutory regulatory codes of conduct and professional practice underpinning biomedicine.

With regard to what Habermas terms the system world and the life world, the wrangle over professional regulation, although based ostensibly on patient safety and raising quality of care (which are clearly crucial), is a vehicle through which 'the systems world is able to re-colonise' aspects of the life world that have threatened to become uncoupled from it. Yet, as Giddens' orientation towards late modernity would suggest, the idea of reflexive society also reminds us that agents and social movements are resistant to such colonisations. Habermas might suggest that this resistance is more reformist than we sometimes like to think, because it is fundamentally concerned with reining back and reinvigorating orthodox system imperatives and articulating them with other, disparate values, practices and ideas associated with the 'life world', rather than with abandoning orthodoxy per se. In this sense, the tension between orthodox medicine and CAM is not so much one of either biomedicine or CAM, but rather between the full *incorporation* of CAM and/or CAM's *integration* with biomedicine.

Conclusion

In summary, CAM poses a number of challenges to medical orthodoxy. Firstly, as argued, CAM's growing popularity from below is partly fuelled by the rejection of orthodox medicine and the search for more holistic, person-centred and less invasive treatments and therapies. Giddens' emphasis on the reflexive potentials inherent in late modernity seems to offer scope for articulating this challenge in terms of the erosion of traditional structures and the opening up of new structures that agents must negotiate more critically and reflexively. However, the tension between 'life' and 'system' worlds, to which Habermas draws our attention, as well as Weber's approach to professional power, suggests that it would be wrong to see this challenge as one based simply on the rejection of orthodox medicine in preference for CAM. Rather, it would be more realistic to think of it in terms of a struggle to integrate the best aspects of CAM with those of biomedicine and, by so doing, saving biomedicine from an uncoupled systems world by re-coupling it with the values and practices associated with the life world. This latter tension provides the basis also for understanding the role of the state as being in a condition of tension between *incorporation* and *integration* of biomedicine and CAMs. When system imperatives of cost-cutting, efficiency and administration are uppermost, then the state leans towards attempting to impose abstract managerial discourses across CAMs, which take less account of the particularities of their individual practices and skill sets and more account of the need to shadow the administrative fiat of orthodoxy. However, when 'life world' imperatives gain a voice, this can be seen in the extent to which the state is genuinely searching for professional codes of conduct and training that are sensitive to the specifics of the alternative medicine they are designed to regulate and that recognise the underpinning philosophy that comes with alternative medicine, rather than expunging its holistic philosophy for a reworked Cartesian dualism.

In both cases, the potential is there for the influence of medicine per se to grow in society. One could argue that the integration of complementary and alternative medicines with orthodox medicine broadens the threshold of medicine in society, under the guiding influence of medical science and the state. As the threshold broadens, the possibility for it to become more diffuse also arises, due in part to the plurality of medicines in play across society which the integration of alternatives into orthodoxy implies. Under this conceptual scenario there is the possibility of a more diffuse medicalisation of society, one increasingly decoupled from the institutions of medicine, and thus one that increasingly invades everyday language as a means of making sense of the day-to-day experiences we encounter in social life (Furedi, 2004). As Conrad notes, 'Medicalisation is not limited to defining conditions where medicine over-steps juridical boundaries into non-medical matters, but now has a more pervasive influence', which 'consists of defining a problem in medical terms, using medical language to describe a problem, adopting a medical framework to understand a problem, or using a medical intervention to "treat" it' (Conrad, 1992, cited in Davis, 2006, p 53). The next chapter follows this line of thinking, through a discussion of the growing preoccupation with happiness, therapy and counselling.

Questions for further reflection

1   Identify what you understand to be the five key points of late modernity.
2   Make a brief outline (no more than half a page) of what you would understand Illich's explanation of the growing popularity of complementary and alternative medicines to be.
3   Identify five key points of difference between how Giddens and Habermas understand late modernity.

References

Armstrong, D. (2002) 'The rise of medical surveillance', in S. Nettleton and U. Gustaffson (eds) *The sociology of health and illness reader*, Cambridge: Polity.

Allsop, J. (2006) 'Regaining trust in medicine: professional and state strategies', *Current Sociology*, vol 54, no 4, pp 621-36.

Aston, R. (2001) 'Rise in popularity of complementary and alternative medicine: reasons and consequences for vaccination', *Vaccine*, pp S90-S93.

British Medical Association (BMA) (1992) 'Report on alternative medicine', in M. Saks (ed) *Alternative medicine in Britain*, Oxford: Clarendon Press.

BMA (1993) *Complementary medicine: New approaches to good practice*, Oxford: Oxford University Press.

Bodeker, G. and Kronenberg, F. (2002) 'A public health agenda for traditional, complementary, and alternative medicine', *American Journal of Public Health*, vol 92, no 10, pp 1582-91.

British Medical Journal (2001) Editorial, vol 322, pp 154-8.

Cant, S. and Sharma, U. (1998) *A new medical pluralism? Doctors, patients and the state*, London: Routledge.

Cant, S. and Sharma, U. (2002) 'The state and complementary medicine', in S. Nettleton and U. Gustafsson (eds) *The sociology of health and illness reader*, Cambridge: Polity.

Davis, J.E. (2006) 'How medicalization lost its way', *Society*, vol 43, no 6, pp 51–6.

Department of Health (2001) *Government Response to the House of Lords Select Committee Report on Complementary and Alternative Medicine*, March, London: Department of Health.

Ernst, E. (2000) 'The role of complementary and alternative medicine', *British Medical Journal*, vol 321, pp 1133-5.

Eysenbach, G. et al (1999) 'Shopping around the internet today and tomorrow: towards the millennium of cybermedicine', *British Medical Journal*, vol 319, pp 1-5.

Fadlon, J. (2004) 'Meridians, chakras and psycho-neuro-immunology: the dematerializing body and the domestication of alternative medicine', *Body & Society*, vol 10, no 4, pp 69–86.

Fennell, D. et al (2009) 'Definitions and patterns of CAM use by the lay public', *Complementary Therapies in Medicine*, vol 17, pp 71–7.

Frank, A.W. (2000) 'Illness and autobiographical work: dialogue as narrative destabilization', *Qualitative Sociology*, vol 23, no 1, pp 135–56.

Friedson, E. (1988) *Profession of medicine: A study of the sociology of applied knowledge*, Chicago, IL: Chicago University Press.

Fulder, S. (1996) *The handbook of alternative and complementary medicine, Part 1*, Oxford: Oxford Medical Press.

Furedi, F. (2004) 'How did we get here?', in F. Furedi, *Therapy culture: Cultivating vulnerability in an uncertain age*, London: Routledge.

Gabe, J. et al (1994) *Challenging medicine*, London: Routledge.

Giddens, A. (1991) *Modernity and self-identity: Self and society in the late modern age*, Cambridge, Polity Press.

Goode, L. (2005) *Jurgen Habermas: Democracy and the public sphere*, London: Pluto Press.

Habermas, J. (1971) *Theory of communicative action, Volume 1, Reason and the rationalisation of society*, Cambridge: Polity Press.

Habermas, J. (1978) *Knowledge and human interests*, trans J.J. Shapiro, Boston, MA: Beacon.

Habermas, J. (1987) *The theory of communicative action, Volume II, Lifeworld and system: a critique of functionalist reason*, trans T. McCarthy, Boston, MA: Beacon.

Heaphy, B. (2007) *Late modernity and social change*, London: Routledge.

Hollenberg, D. (2006) 'Uncharted ground: Patterns of professional interaction among complementary/alternative and biomedical practitioners in integrative health care settings', *Social Science & Medicine*, vol 62, no 3, February, pp 731–44.

House of Lords (2002) *House of Lords Select Committee on Science and Technology Sixth Report: Complementary and alternative medicine*, London: HMSO.

Kleinman, A. and Seeman, D. (2000) 'Personal experience of illness', in G.L. Albrecht et al (eds), *The handbook of social studies in medicine*, London: Sage.

Lash, S. (1999) *Another modernity, a different rationality*, Oxford: Blackwell Publishers.

Lawrence, C. (1994) *Medicine in the making of modern Britain, 1700–1920*, London: Routledge.

Mintel International Group Ltd (2005) *Complementary medicines – UK*, Pub ID: Gno 1099196 (March), London: Mintel.

NCCAM (National Center for Complementary and Alternative Medicine) (2009) (www.libraryindex.com/pages/56/Alternative-Medicine.html), accessed 2 March 2009.

Newton, J.R. et al (2008) 'Use of complementary and alternative medicine by patients attending a head and neck oncology clinic', *The Journal of Laryngology and Otology*, vol 122, pp 1360–4.

Oakley, A. (1993) *Women, medicine and health*, Edinburgh: Edinburgh University Press.

Porter, R. (1997) *The greatest benefit to mankind: A medical history of humanity from antiquity to the present*, London: Harper Collins.

Prior, L. (2003) 'Belief, knowledge and expertise: the emergence of the lay expert in medical sociology', *Sociology of Health and Illness*, vol 25, no 3, pp 41–57.

Roberts, M.J.D. (2009) 'The politics of professionalization: MPs, medical men, and the 1858 Medical Act, *Medical History*, vol 53, no 1, pp 37–56.

Saks, M. (1994) 'The alternatives to medicine', in J. Gabe et al (eds) *Challenging medicine,* London: Routledge.

Thomas, K. and Coleman, P. (2004) 'Use of complementary or alternative medicine in a general population in Great Britain. Results from the National Omnibus survey', *Journal of Public Health*, vol 26, no 2, pp 152–7.

Thomas, K. et al (2008) 'Developing research strategies in complementary and alternative medicine', *Complementary Therapies in Medicine*, vol 16, pp 359–62.

Velanovich, V. et al (2006) 'Patterns of usage of complementary and alternative medicine in general surgical patients', *International Journal of Surgery*, vol 4, pp 206–11.

Ward, P.R. (2006) 'Trust, reflexivity and dependence: a "social systems theory" analysis in/of medicine', *European Journal of Social Quality*, vol 6, no 2, pp 143–58.

Weber, M. (1978) *Economy and society: An outline of interpretive sociology*, ed G. Roth and C. Wittich, Berkeley, CA: University of California Press.

WHO (World Health Organisation) (2002) *Traditional medicine strategy, 2002–2005*, World Health Organisation: Geneva.

Williams, G. and Popay, J. (1994) 'Lay knowledge and the privilege of experience', in J. Gabe et al (eds) *Challenging medicine*, London: Routledge.

Williams, S.J. and Calnan, M. (1996) 'The limits of medicalisation?: Modern medicine and the lay populace in "late modernity"', *Social Science and Medicine*, vol 42, no 12, pp 1609–20.

FOUR

The happiness and self-help industry

If counselling is the 'new religion', therapy and anti-depressants must be the new opiates of the people. Confession, once the realm of the priest, is now bread and butter for the therapist. And with the demise of the old spiritual leaders we have new gurus, offering absolution and advice through the media. (Caroline Daniel, 1997)

Every city should have a policy for promoting a healthier philosophy of life in its youngsters and for helping them to distinguish between a hedonistic addiction to superficial pleasures and real happiness. (Layard, 2005b)

Evolution favors a happiness function that measures the individual's success in relative terms. The optimal function is based on a time-varying reference point—or performance benchmark—that is updated over time in a statistically optimal way in order to match the individual's potential. (Becker and Rayo, 2007, p 2)

Introduction

Happiness has become a central issue in recent years – especially the concern to define it, how we might measure it and whether we can improve levels of happiness across society, and so on. Academics, health professionals and governments now explore the minutiae of the conditions for happiness; the psychological predispositions for attaining happiness; the relationship between happiness and prosperity; happiness and health, and so on. This search for happiness is closely associated with the prevalence of personal counselling services throughout society and the burgeoning interest in therapies like cognitive behavioural therapy, client-centred therapy, goal-directed therapy; relationship therapy; emotional therapy; anger management counselling; therapies to enhance emotional intelligence, and so on. Bookshops also display a wealth of books on happiness and well-being that offer advice on how to transform one's present miseries and learn to live the good life.

   This chapter first considers the growing preoccupation with improving happiness and well-being, and how this is linked to the rise of a new and novel happiness industry whose product is therapy, 'lifestyle coaching' and the management of individual and interpersonal relations. The chapter then relates the happiness and therapy industry to broader social changes associated with high modernity, and assesses the role that a blossoming happiness and therapy industry plays within a context of sustained social inequality. The context of widening social inequality sets the agenda for evaluating the view that the 'happiness industry' and pervasive culture of therapy advance the forces of medicalisation in more diffuse and powerful ways. We invoke the relationship between a pervasive culture of therapy and the wider cultural shifts associated with late modernity in order to assess the ways in which relationships become increasingly mediated in terms of the personal, the psychological and the emotive, and less in terms of the collective bonds between people.

The happiness and self-help industry

Richard Layard, the Labour peer and Professor of Economic Policy at the London School of Economics, has written a book on the 'science of happiness' (Layard, 2005a), in part to address the following apparent conundrum:

> Over the last 50 years, we in the west have enjoyed unparalleled economic growth. We have better homes, cars, holidays, jobs, education and above all health. According to standard economic theory, this should have made us happier. But surveys show otherwise. When Britons or Americans are asked how happy they are, they report no improvement over the last 50 years. More people suffer from depression, and crime – another indicator of dissatisfaction – is also much higher. (Layard, 2005, p 1)

According to a global study (World Values Survey, 2003, cited by Gunnel, 2004) which tracked the attitudes of people in 65 countries over 12 years to 2001, once one rises above the relatively low gross income threshold of $13,000 (at 1995 purchasing power), then the extra money received does not make people significantly happier. Obviously there is a large slice of subjectivity here – that is, what do we mean by 'significantly'? Is it the same for all classes and cultures? Leaving these questions aside for the moment, it would appear to be the case that, while being poor can certainly make you miserable, and gaining more income when you are poor can certainly make you happier, once one is able to secure basic needs, then more and more money simply does not have anywhere near the same impact on levels of happiness. According to the World Values Survey (2003, cited by Gunnel, 2004), the US is the world's richest country by far, yet is only the 13th happiest of the 65 countries measured in the global survey.

As mentioned briefly in the introduction to this chapter, government policy in the UK has increasingly adopted the language of well-being and happiness. The National Statistical Office is developing measurements of well-being. The rolling out of cognitive behaviour therapy (CBT) by the Department of Health and the emphasis placed on the social and emotional aspects of learning by the Department of Schools and Families are further evidence of a 'happiness' agenda that has entered the level of public policy in the UK (Jeffries, 2008). In 2000 a journal dedicated to the study of happiness, the *Journal of Happiness Studies*, was founded, and it has produced advances in our understanding of how happiness can be experienced differently across time and cultures, and how concepts of happiness relate to or are compatible with 'the good life', and so on. Of course, happiness means many different things to different people and so there is no absolute basis for measurement. However, from the point of view of this book, what is more interesting is our growing preoccupation with whether or not, or to what degree, we are happy and with debating what happiness could actually mean.

This growing preoccupation with seeking happiness or worrying about why we are not happier and, indeed, about what happiness actually means, appears to have connections with a growing industry involved in the production of 'happiness drugs' and with a range of diverse forms of therapy, personal counselling and lifestyle coaching, and so on. For example, the preoccupation with happiness 'by other means' may be observed in medicine's willingness to prescribe serotonin. Serotonin is the brain chemical associated with happiness, and the new-generation (designer) drugs currently on the market are selective serotonin reuptake inhibitors (SSRIs). In Britain in 1995, 13.2 million prescriptions were written for antidepressants in general. By 2002 this figure had doubled for SSRIs alone (Gunnell, 2004). Globally, this kind of medication now generates roughly $17 billion a year for the pharmaceutical industry. If we combine this with other behavioural drugs, the (legal) 'lifestyle drugs' market as a whole is thought to be worth $23 billion annually.

The search for happiness and the emphasis on how increasingly stressful life has become have provided two major platforms upon which a therapeutic outlook has flourished, complete with the overly optimist quick-fix-kit solution that appears to have invaded more areas of everyday living. In Odone's more colourful turn of phrase, we have apparently developed a penchant for embracing the 'Disney-style optimism and positive mind-set of American self-help gurus who, from Jane Fonda to Deepak Chopra, taught us that sad was bad. Their feel-good philosophies raised our expectations of happiness – and lowered our pain threshold: the slightest headache sent us to the medicine cabinet, the merest twinge of melancholy to the therapist, and the tiniest slight made us erupt in expletive-spitting rage.' Would we put up with anything less than perfect contentment? It would appear not, for, as Odonne continues, 'Brainwashed by a culture which said happiness was the natural state of being, we turned to everything from homeopathic herbs to Tantric yoga, from the television confessional to the psychiatrist's chair to rid our lives of disturbing thoughts' (Odone, 1999).

Odone may be accused of hyperbole, but her core point is that we live in a culture where individuals increasingly articulate their emotions through therapy, and that the language of therapy rings true. Rowe (2000) observes how, as a nation, we seem to be increasingly preoccupied by those imponderable but ever-so-interesting questions such as: 'Am I happy? Why can't I be happy? Shouldn't I be happier than I am? These are questions that nowadays seem to plague us'. It would seem that the search for happiness brings about its own form of uncertainty and discontent. Such questions suggest that, as a society, we are plagued by the need to search for personal fulfilment and happiness. It would seem that the more we have and we own, the more we feel alone, the more we become discontented with our lot – searching for the holy grail of happiness and inner peace. Celebrity culture no doubt plays a part by fostering images of the unhappy rich and famous seeking the holy grail of happiness – fostering the view that money cannot buy happiness, and so an acceptance of one's place in society (Holderman, 2007, p 288).

This search for happiness has fuelled a 'happiness industry' in which happiness and therapeutic entrepreneurs have flourished, claiming to provide '10 easy-to-follow steps' towards fulfilment and the like. The growth in the demand for and supply of psychotherapy and counselling has developed most in the US, where it is a well-established and ever-expanding multi-billion dollar industry. According to Dunoway (2000), the US Department of Health and Human Services estimated that by 1999 the healthcare market for traditional psychotherapy and counselling services was valued at $70 billion.

Demand for personal counselling and therapy in the UK is also expanding. According to a survey completed in 2004, one in five UK citizens has had psychotherapy or counselling. The survey also found that more than eight in 10 people now think therapy is acceptable in certain circumstances. Almost two-thirds said they knew someone who could benefit from therapy, and it is estimated that 250,000 people now offer services in counselling and psychotherapy across the UK. In this sense, therapy 'has gained mass acceptance in the more emotionally "in touch" Britain of 2004. Not only has the concept gained acceptance but it has become a practical reality for a significant minority, with 21% of the population having personal experience of therapy' (Future Foundation, 2004).

Moreover, although there are currently moves to regulate the therapy industry (Department of Health, 2007), it remains the case today that the professional boundaries within counselling and therapeutic services are increasingly blurred, allowing entry to practitioners of different levels of expertise and qualification. For example, a derivative of our apparently therapy-reliant age is the huge growth in popularity of life or lifestyle coaching. Lifestyle coaching extends therapy from the couch to the management of everyday aspects of our life and work. While psychotherapists train to diagnose our emotional or cognitive disorders, frequently delving into the past to help clients understand their behaviour, resolve problems and relieve psychological pain, life coaches cater to our apparent need for personal assistance in bringing focus and emotional perspective to our lives and, as the spiel goes, help us to 'realise our potential at work and as human beings in general'. Lifestyle coaching, it could be argued, may offer a means of seeking psychotherapy without the associated stigma that psychotherapy has for many people. In particular, it can often be a more socially acceptable way for adult males to acquire therapy, conjuring up as it does images of the 'coach' in sport and the masculinities this symbolises. Lifestyle coaching also gets a 'good press' because of its relationship with industry and employer–employee relations.

In this sense, lifestyle coaching is a derivative of the 'soft skills' said to be involved in the 'human resources' or personnel management industry.

As was intimated above, the turn towards the language of lifestyle coaching rather than therapy allows one to practise and provide a service without the rigours of professional qualifications usually ascribed to psychiatry. For although it is argued that the two (psychotherapy and lifestyle coaching) are separate, there is a very large grey area in the relationships and behaviours they both deal with. In particular, the search for happiness, empowerment and therapeutic solutions criss-crosses the psychotherapy/lifestyle coaching divide, making the boundaries difficult to discern, especially for clients/patients/consumers.

The porosity of the boundaries has certainly enabled the growth of this industry. In 2002 there were an estimated 500 lifestyle coaches in Britain. By the end of 2004 that figure had risen to around 4,000 (Thompson, 2005). Amazon reported a 38% rise in its top five lifestyle coaching titles (Thompson, 2005). It is claimed that in Edinburgh, demand for lifestyle coaching was so high that the Department of Lifelong Learning at Edinburgh University was offering evening programmes about life coaching (MacEacheran, 2004). And Glasgow, voted the most stressful place to live in the UK in 2004, became a hotbed of therapists and lifestyle gurus offering the dream of a better life (MacEacheran, 2004). Such is the demand for lifestyle coaching that, as one journalist put it, 'Britain has a new motto for 2005: don't get a life, get a life coach' (Thompson, 2005).

Unsurprisingly, lifestyle coaching is a very lucrative business. MacEacheran pointed out that an experienced coach could charge upwards of £300 a month and could make £40,000–£60,000 per year (MacEacheran, 2004). As the potential earnings grow, so too does the demand for training future therapists. The UK now has its very own UK College of Lifestyle Coaching, responding to increased consumer demand for coaching: 'The ever-increasing awareness of life coaching among the general population and the vast amount of media coverage ranging from magazines to television programmes, has seen a continuous increase in the demand for Life Coaches in the UK' (MacEacheran, 2004).

Life coaching, reasons the College, entails working with people who already have a measure of 'success' in their lives, 'but who want to bridge the gap between where they are and where they want to be in their profession and their personal life ... When you empower a person and show him what he can do – instead of focusing on what he can't do (weakness) – you can improve his overall mental health and his life dramatically' (Institute of Life Coaching, 2003). Promising to increase economic success, improve health, improve communication skills and enhance personality, then it is small wonder that the life coaching industry is a £billion industry in the UK today (Dee, 2010).

This message is also driven home to the wider population via the proliferation of self-help books, magazines, journals and TV programmes. In the US alone, 'Between 3500 and 4000 new self-help books appeared in 2003 ... more than double the number in 1998 ..., anchored by a spate of musings [with titles such as] *The Purpose Driven Life*; *Your Best Life Now*; *7 Steps to Living at Your Full Potential*;

and various tomes about the "giant who slumbers within you" and the 6 dozen separate chicken soup books now in print' (Salerno, 2005, p 8).

The UK is fast catching up. The self-help book market was estimated to be worth about £80 million in 2004 (Gunnell, 2004). Enter any major high street bookshop today and you cannot fail to notice shelf after shelf of books offering advice on the fastest route to happiness or the 10 most important self-help tips for achieving the good life.

Why the preoccupation with happiness and therapy?

Having outlined the contours of a growing happiness industry, we now turn to consider the reasons for this growth, through a discussion of competing conceptual frameworks. We begin with the argument that the happiness and self-help industry is a mass fraud held together by profitability, the power of the media and the gullibility of individuals wanting easy remedies for the normal problems of everyday living (Salerno, 2005).

Salerno argues that the happiness industry is a sham industry feeding on the decline in traditional society. For Salerno, the traditional family based around the 'male breadwinner model' provided the building blocks of shared norms and values that gave individuals a proper sense of their place in the world. These shared norms and values also reflected a period when there was much more healthy realism about medicine and healthcare and what individuals could and could not achieve healthwise. In *traditional society* we 'knew our place' in the social hierarchy, while understanding that, through our own efforts, we could be upwardly social mobile.

Yet all this has been threatened. Increasing divorce rates and broken homes reflect moral decay, in the sense that individuals are less willing to take responsibility for their lives and the lives of others; they seek the easy way out. Moreover, the lack of employment and work experience has left large parts of society bereft of the work ethic. Alongside this has been the growth in consumerism, in which we measure ourselves by what we can buy, not who we are as persons, and this is further fuelled by the media, which often portray our lives through images of idols and icons living out fantasy lives.

Into this fray the happiness industry emerges, controlled by charlatans capitalising on the social woes that result from the breakdown of traditional society. The charlatans inhabiting the world of the self-help industries prey on individuals by offering them the appearance of an easy, quick fix to the problems encountered as a result of the breakdown of traditional social order. Salerno argues that the happiness industry preys on the increasing number of individuals who fall under its beguiling spell in two opposing but related ways: through discourses of *victimhood* and of *empowerment*.

Salerno claims that individuals are turned into *victims* when the industry plays down the ability of people to make real changes to their environment and when it plays up the view that people are victims of their biology or cultural background. This appears to be opposite to what the industry emphasises: it is all about 'self'-help. Yet the self-help is really a cover for relinquishing one's own powers of self-help to others, to be 'managed' as they see appropriate. For example, 'anger management' and various forms of therapy ask individuals to leave their own accounts of why they are angry or in need of therapy at the door, and to embrace preconceived programmes of 'managed therapy'. Moreover, argues Salerno, victimhood is reinforced by a self-help industry that takes every opportunity to instil a sense of guilt and fatalism into individuals. The industry's role is to exhort individuals to snap out of their self-imposed lethargy, self-loathing and self-pity. Under the banner of slogans such as 'It isn't your fault', 'You gotta let go of the guilt', 'I'm dysfunctional you're dysfunctional', the clear message for the victim is that it was not their fault, they must think of their own welfare, not of others' (the 'me, me' philosophy) and redefine their values along lines beneficial to the self-help gurus in control of the self-help industry.

> Its moorings sunk in notions of recovery, victimisation theory was embraced by a loose coalition of pop-psychologists, social scientists and academics … who sought to explain every human frailty as a function of some hardwired predisposition or inescapable social root: you were basically trapped by your make up and/or environment and thus had a ready-made alibi for any and all of your failings. (Salerno, 2005, p 30)

The message would appear to be clear: we are helpless before both nature and nurture and require help to manage our lives – enter the self-help and happiness industry!

The paradox, for Salerno, is that the happiness industry also aspires to *empower* individuals. Empowerment refers to situations in which we have decision-making power and have the right to make changes to our lives. However, empowerment can often turn into its opposite – disempowerment – if, in reality, our ability to make decisions is constrained and frustrated by situations we have little or no control over. Salerno argues that the happiness industry disempowers people under the guise of empowerment, because it makes unrealistic demands on people's ability to change. The industry ignores wider inequalities of class, gender, ethnicity, age or disability. All you require is the right attitude, the right life coach manager, or the most appropriate form of psychotherapy, and you can be who you want to be; you can aspire to reach your ideal goals and realise all of your dreams, regardless of social circumstance.

Salerno (2005) may have a point here; the internet makes available hundreds of counselling and therapy solutions which offer the most far-reaching positive outcomes to those who would embark on their courses of therapy and self-help formulas. One finds little by way of acknowledgement of the social constraints that make change difficult, and so potentially place it beyond the control of the individual. Instead, the emphasis is on assuring consumers that by taking 12, 10 or even just five steps they have the potential to dismiss past failures and phobias and spirit away future social obstacles.

One limitation of Salerno's account is that it is one-sided; he chooses to ignore any evidence that presents the self-help industry in a positive light. Another is that his analysis rests on a deeply conservative view of individuals. For example, his criticisms of the self-help industry rest on a view of a golden past when families were nuclear and mum and dad had their gender roles firmly in control and kids knew their place. In this world, people stood on their own two feet and didn't expect handouts from the state through welfare cheques they had never earned. Salerno's argument with the self-help industry is over its promotion of victimhood and a form of so-called empowerment that effectively disempowers people and disables any incentive they might have had to take responsibility for themselves and their own families, to take up a job, compete in the market place and act like good but responsible 'active' citizens.

His view leads Salerno to look for scapegoats in the breakdown of his traditional society, one major culprit being the self-help industry. If we feed this into a broader conceptualisation of the medicalisation thesis, then it can also be seen from Salerno's writings that he sees the 'charlatans' of the self-help industry as acting totally separately from the legal authority of the professional experts who give advice about people's health on the basis of objective traditional medical science. By making an artificial divide between the two, he leaves biomedicine intact and focuses on an industry of charlatans who, he believes, are making a profit out of other people's misery. In this sense, he misses the more fundamental point raised earlier by Furedi, that of the possibility of a more diffuse medicalisation of society, one increasingly decoupled from the institutions of medicine and one that thus increasingly invades everyday language as a means of making sense of the day-to-day experiences we encounter in social life (Furedi, 2004). Arguably, Anthony Giddens (1991) provides a more nuanced account of the wider social context within which the self-help industry emerges. It is useful, therefore, to offer Giddens as a counter-weight to Salerno.

Anthony Giddens and the self-help industry in 'high modernity'

Anthony Giddens is known for his writings on how individuals shape wider society and how, in reverse, society shapes and influences the actions of individuals. He is particularly interested in how current changes in modern ways of living influence and sometimes shape our lives, for better or worse. Although Giddens does not directly explore the self-help and happiness industry, his concern with the 'individual–society' dynamic, in the context of what he describes as the shift from *traditional* society to *high modernity*, does offer a useful explanation as to why the self-help and psychotherapy industries have become so popular in recent decades (Giddens, 1991).

As we outlined in Chapter Three, Giddens (1991) argues that we are currently living through a transition from traditional society to a society in which relationships are more stretched, dispersed and socially mobile, which he refers to as 'high modernity'. We noted in Chapter Three in particular that under conditions of high modernity individuals experience insecurities and opportunities due to a number of changes pivotal to the society, such as a marked increase in rates of divorce since the 1960s, the emergence of diverse family structures, erosion of the male breadwinner model, flexible modes of employment, often leading to more insecure employment contracts, and the necessity to multi-skill and adapt to lifelong learning; all of which are bound up with uncertainties relating to identity.

For Giddens, the changes signify role ambiguity, uncertainty, social fluidity and a more reflexive awareness of risks and potential opportunities as older forms of social stratification become redefined, open up avenues of escape or new avenues of oppression. Accentuating the more optimistic side of high modernity leads Giddens to the view that we all become much more aware that our lives can be transformed by our own actions; more aware of our own role and the role that others can play in reshaping our social worlds. We no longer *have* a biography, we *live* our biography.

It is in the context of ambiguity and uncertainty, generated by the shift towards high modernity, that one can perhaps understand the focus on happiness and the development of the self-help industry. On this reading, they emerge out of insecurities and risks, as well as from the opportunities for self-advancement associated with the above social changes. The growth of the self-help and happiness industry is, accordingly, both in response to individuals who are committed to actively seeking to reconstruct and shape their own identities, to take control of their biographies, and a response to the deep insecurities individuals experience as a result of major life changes – which can often leave them vulnerable, and susceptible to a happiness industry that demonstrates 12 quick steps to happiness and contentment. In this respect, Giddens (1991) notes how the uncertainty in an individual's life can often demand *psychic reorganisation*. For example, when large-scale social change takes place, traditional meaning systems no longer work so well to integrate individuals; gaps develop between individuals and social systems which demand a 'psychic reorganisation', or, in other words, a means by which the individual can manage the changes to their identity. The rise of therapy culture and the self-help and happiness industry is very much a part of such a 'psychic reorganisation'. According to this view, it is not an industry of prophets carving out profits by deceiving vast numbers of individuals who have been duped into doling out money for phoney solutions to social problems. Although this is very much one facet of the industry, it also offers something genuine. Following Giddens, one could argue that the industry is responding to a more active citizenry. The self-help industry, with its complement of life coaching, counselling and psychotherapy cures and solutions to everyday life, is a response to the demands of individuals seeking new ways of living and new systems of meaning that give purpose to their lives; it serves, in other words, as a means through which individuals give shape and direction to their own biographies.

While Giddens presents a more nuanced assessment of the self-help industry, he also tends to play down how the same trends have alienated individuals and weakened their social ties. For example, Layard (2005b), who would otherwise agree with the main thrust of Giddens' view of high modernity, also points out that the rise of the happiness and counselling industry is a by-product of market capitalism, which has encouraged the pursuit of money and consumerism and discouraged community values, which have become weakened by possessive individualism in the race to acquire material goods. For Layard, individuals have been encouraged to seek salvation in money rather than in social relations. High modernity may mean that society as a whole may be economically better off, but the economic rat race for larger incomes, money and consumer goods per se leads to a stress on work over leisure, economics over social relations. The race to gain economic status and to consume more, as a means of social ranking, quickly becomes a zero-sum game in which there will always be losers threatened by economic and social exclusion and there will always be winners concerned to maintain their privileged status. As Layard argues, 'when material discomfort has been banished, extra income becomes much less important than our relationships with each other: with family, with friends and in the community. The danger is that we sacrifice relationships too much in pursuit of higher income' (Layard, 2005b, p 1).

Layard's solutions are that policy makers redress the balance between growing gross domestic product (GDP) and economic efficiency, in the direction of a policy that enhances Gross Domestic Happiness and Well-being. Employment relations should foster the goals of team working and collective enterprise; education ought to factor in social skills, collective values and the centrality of moral obligation towards others.

Paradoxically, there is a passing similarity between Layard and Salerno. Layard, like Salerno, lays emphasis on fostering traditional values. However, Layard, unlike Salerno, views status hierarchies as detrimental to the objective of increasing the general level of happiness and societal well-being; for Salerno, to know one's place is a mark of contentment. Layard would agree with Giddens that the economic and personal freedoms said to result from high modernity have been for the good. Where he departs from Giddens is in emphasising work–family–life balance. Money, income, working hard and consumption are important to happiness, but not if they become the sole activity or squeeze out other areas of life that make for a more rounded person; there needs to be a balance between money-making and commodity consumption and spending, the time and skills required to develop interpersonal relations, foster and develop community spirit, and so on.

However, there are significant omissions from Layard's account, and bringing them to light reveals how both Layard's and Giddens' conceptual frameworks effectively serve to medicalise our understanding of, and so possible solutions to, deeply ingrained social inequalities. For clearly, behind the discovery of an inverse relation between material wealth and levels of happiness are issues of ingrained and long-term poverty, the persistence of insecure and poorly paid employment, the intensification of work and the growing chasm between the rich and the rest of society. Both Giddens and Layard tend to ignore the growing chasm in favour of individualistic accounts of movement between social exclusion and inclusion. As two of the main intellectual architects of the Labour government's New Deal and Welfare to Work programmes, both Giddens and Layard have promoted employment as a significant opportunity to escape from the isolation and poverty-inducing effects of unemployment. Yet the life-enhancing quality of the kind of employment opportunities associated with the latter programme is debatable. Linked to a stricter benefit regime bequeathed from the previous Conservative government, the New Deal and Welfare to Work programmes have been centrally concerned with generating 'employability', not so much with guaranteeing employment. And when employment is the driver, adopting an employment-first policy has tended to emphasise the development of training programmes and skills acquisition necessary for the kind of low–skill, low–status, poorly paid and insecure employment that may actually increase the sum of unhappiness (Finn, 2000; Peck and Theodore, 2000). Indeed, part and parcel of the Labour government's broader policy strategy has been to 'subordinate social policy to the alleged economic imperatives of global competition' (Jessop, 2006, p 9).

With regard to poverty, 'On the standard measure of poverty, 60% of median income, the percentage of individuals in households below the poverty line after housing costs rose from around 14% in 1979 to nearly 25% as Labour took office in 1997. By 2007, despite a ten-year period of sustained economic expansion, the poverty line had only fallen 20%'. If we consider those in severe poverty (40% of the medium income), they have experienced stagnation. Moreover, 'Poverty amongst working-age adults without dependent children is now at its highest level since records began in 1961' (IFS, 2009, p 2). Meanwhile the disparity between those living in poverty and the rich continues to rise. 'Over the period since 2004–05, the incomes of the poorest fifth of households have fallen by 2.6%, after inflation, while the incomes of the richest fifth rose by nearly 3.3% on the same basis' (IFS, 2009, p 3). On the one hand, it is difficult to see how Giddens can express such optimism concerning the economic and social changes which have led to the above disparities. On the other hand, it is very difficult to reconcile the kinds of solutions for increasing happiness and well-being that Layard promotes, when faced with the structurally ingrained nature of such inequalities.

What the above overview of social inequalities and their enduring nature does explain, perhaps, is a material understanding of why happiness levels are not keeping pace with high modernity. As Ferguson (2006) reflects, those who draw attention to rises in average living standards 'seldom look at what else has been going on in the lives of millions of people during the same period, which broadly coincides with the implementation of neoliberal policies'. Members of the British Association for Counselling and Psychotherapy (BACP), for example, would quite reasonably claim that they have the best interests of their clients in mind and are keen to acknowledge the importance of social inequalities. However, they tend to ignore the wider economic and social processes involved in those social inequalities and emphasise instead the role of wider values, such as acquisitiveness, greed and narcissism, in driving this inequality and, as a consequence, are far less socially effective and indirectly serve the status quo. As Morrell (2009) argues,

> the ability of an individual to change his/her personal circumstances through therapy is dictated, limited, or moulded by 'social power'. Social power is external to and beyond the influence of the client. Potent factors in the manufacture of social power on the individual include the influence of close family and friends, but are primarily the physical environment, general attitudes and prejudices, organisational allegiances and, crucially, the actions of those in government, those who run global corporations, and those who head up military oligarchies.

Morrell suggests that the way forward for the therapy industry is to shift away from preoccupation with the 'self', decoupled from the commercialisation of happiness, and to align more directly and actively with social movements of the oppressed. However, Morrell gives less indication about how such a transformation should come about. This lacuna, argues Furedi (2004), leaves a situation in which the self-help and therapy industry encourages and supports a preoccupation with personal therapy and a growing tacit acceptance of such inequalities as inevitable constraints, which in turn lead inwards, and a preoccupation with the pursuit of self-change through new consumer identities.

Furedi, therapy culture and the self-help industry

Furedi argues that therapy culture feeds upon a society in which the major preoccupation is with one's self and less with the community. In other words, therapy culture develops rapidly under conditions of extreme individualism, where self-interest spills over easily into self-obsession with bodily matters, to the exclusion of concerns about broader social change. Furedi draws attention to the decline of collective forms of politics. The decline in the number of people turning out to vote in general elections has been one manifestation of this; as is the decline in class-based politics, which has been emphasised in Britain by the renaming of the Labour Party as New Labour. The Labour Party grew out of the trade union movement and depended on the working classes for its vote; New Labour depended increasingly upon the middle classes and the ex-Tory vote to win elections. Perhaps more crucially, the reasons for the decline in politics are due to the decline in political ideologies. Ideologies are sets of ideas about the ways in which society ought to develop that provide a vision of social progress and of what ought to be that is greater than the individual. Ideologies inspire individuals to look to social change rather than to personality change in order to exact a better life.

The demise of ideology is thus also the demise of visions about larger social purpose, and the vacuum is filled by internalising solutions to social problems, in the form of personal therapy and self-fulfilment. The 19th and 20th centuries provided the context for fierce competition between rival ideologies. Socialism rivalled liberalism's emphasis on the individual in the struggle to bring about a social world in which collective solidarity was central to how individuals lived and prospered. As these collective ideologies, which advanced the cause of the Labour movement, have declined, so too have the collective power and influence of the trade union movement. Nowadays, one is just as likely to be offered counselling by trade unions and employee representatives as advice about how to embark on a collective response to management; whereas once anger at job loss, redundancy and work intensification could be collectivised and directed at managers and employers, today that anger is 'managed' and 'depoliticised' through a range of therapy services, including 'anger management', 'post-redundancy counselling' and the like.

Moreover, in a context in which individuals are increasingly atomised and depoliticised, and so estranged from collective relations with each other – and in fact are encouraged to be so by governments that insist upon the active, independent citizen as opposed to the dependency culture – the role of professionals becomes crucial. Professionals become the core mediators integrating individuals into society.

> The development of modern society has had a profound impact on the conduct of everyday life. Unlike in traditional settings, the modern individual's attachment to others is distinctly fragile and provisional (strangers in a crowd). People's obligations and expectations of one another are often ambiguous and confusing. The continued thinning of communal ties helps foster a sense of depersonalisation. One of the characteristic features of modern times is that the decline of taken for granted ways of doing things has encouraged the perception that individuals are not able to manage important aspects of their own life without professional guidance [and] this has created an opportunity for the 'expert' to colonise the realm of personal relations. (Furedi, 2004, p 98)

Therefore, argues Furedi, alongside the decline in political ideologies, one must also include the 'professionalisation of everyday life' as a powerful motive force in the rise of the self-help and happiness industry.

Furedi refers to this preoccupation with the self and one's relationship with others, framed in the language of therapy and counselling, as a response to the wider *culture of therapy*, which increasingly offers us a way of expressing how we feel about life, helping us to come to terms with the 'inevitableness' of rising social inequalities and social hierarchy. The 'therapist without', so to speak, has a renewed bearing on our innermost relationships, as well as on our roles in society.

Central to therapy culture is the *therapeutic system of meaning*; therapy culture is fast moving from a *sub-cultural* to a *society-wide system of meaning*, as a means of maintaining social order and the means through which individuals understand their situation. The very meaning system crucial to our relationships with others and to the development of our identity and subjectivity is defined increasingly in medical and therapeutic terms. As Furedi reflects,

> The vocabulary of therapeutics no longer refers to unusual problems or exotic states of mind. Terms like stress, anxiety, addiction, compulsion, trauma, negative emotions, healing, syndrome, mid-life crisis or counselling refer to the normal episodes of daily life. They have become part of our cultural imagination. (Furedi, 2004, p 2)

In this way, therapy culture symbolises the medicalisation of life into more areas of society. We get a flavour of the implications of Furedi's argument in the following examples. When passions run high among professional footballers these days, they are told they must seek out a course in 'anger management'. Students in higher education under pressure to pass exams or complete the next essay assignment are more likely to be referred to the student counselling services for 'stress management' or the local student helpline than to their module tutor for intellectual advice; while staff in higher education, faced with the stresses and strains brought on by increasing pressures to teach, research and manage the curriculum are perhaps less likely to view this as a collective employer–employee relation and more likely to view it as resolvable through various individually based 'time management', stress management and counselling courses. If children have problems at school, then there is a tendency towards redefining them in terms of a medical 'problem', amenable to a range of therapies or counselling sessions provided by child specialists. Or if a child should prove to be especially restless in an over-large class, then 'extra assistance' is more likely to be at hand once their behaviour has been redefined in terms of 'attention deficit hyperactive disorder', in need of therapeutic intervention.

Moreover, therapy culture reaches into much broader social and political events. For example, sometimes the primary means by which we come to know, understand and come to terms with the experience of major social tragedies is often framed in the therapeutic terminology of traumas and 'post-traumatic stress', to be managed, understood and brought under control by professionals. The twin tragedies of the Oklahoma bombing in 1994 and the bombing of the World Trade Centre in 2001 provided years of employment for the post-traumatic stress disorder industry. It is often a puzzle that individuals exposed to very different experiences, from football stadium disasters, to the killing sands of the Gulf War, to the mass bombings of inner cities, are all presumed to have the same condition. In all of these examples, argues Furedi, therapy culture serves to conflate the complexity of our relationships and experiences until they can be redefined in the medical terminology of 'prescribed syndromes'.

This 'flattening' of the complexities of social life into personal issues of a medical persuasion is increasingly evident elsewhere, too. Take road accidents, deaths and incidents. We live in a world transfixed by a penchant for private transport and the imperative to build more and more roads to accommodate this, with the car industry acting as a major spur to the road-building and construction industry. Related to this, the pace of work and life, and indeed the distance between work and home, has increased on average every decade since the 1980s. We drive more, we drive faster, have further to travel and live more hectic lives than did previous generations.

It is little wonder that individuals become agitated, frustrated and angry when caught up in traffic jams and facing never-ending deadlines of one type or another to meet. Yet, rather than consider the wider social and economic imperatives driving this situation, we reach for the convenience of a condition affecting certain personalities, which we have labelled 'road-rage', in order to seek out cause and solution. In other words, we prescribe a syndrome. For example, *Psychiatry Today* informs us that 'Psychiatric morbidity and road rage have been linked in several studies'. In particular, 'More recent studies have focused on psychiatric problems in more serious instances of road rage', such as 'Intermittent explosive disorder', which is an 'Axis I diagnosis whose core feature is episodes of aggression that result in serious assaults or property destruction'. As there is no clear link between 'road rage' and 'Intermittent explosive disorder' we are also informed that 'road rage' could equally be triggered by 'Attention Deficit Hyperactive Disorder (ADHD)', especially if you are young, male and a student who happens to drive a car (Reginald et al, 2005)!

Conclusion

This chapter has been concerned with understanding the rise of a very peculiar industry, the self-help and happiness industry. It has provided evidence of the extent to which it has had influence across society, and has considered a number of sociological contributions to helping us understand the nature of this industry and its origins and potential lines of future development. The self-help industry is a huge money spinner for those involved, and its market is continually expanding as more people flock to its remedies and advice. Critics are surely correct to highlight some of the darker sides to this industry and the manipulative ways in which people's emotions and trust serve as the raw material for its profits. The argument that it is more than just an industry, and much more fundamental, owes its origins and continued growth to its role in 'medically mediating' social relations across society, and is also intuitively appealing. We don't have to look far in our own experiences to see how extensive is this tendency to psychologise and personalise what are social problems often beyond individual powers to control. Any 'anger management course' or 'lifestyle coaching experience' we may happen to take may or may not have positive outcomes, but it is surely disingenuous to spirit away the social inequalities and imbalances of power that often underpin personal problems, yet this is what the self-help industry tends to do.

The above highlights the way medicalisation spread out from traditional medical institutions to develop its powers of circulation within the capillaries of society. In this sense, while the previous chapter revealed the broadening of medicalisation across orthodox and alternative medicines and the state as the legitimating agency with powers to integrate CAM, this chapter has considered ways in which this broadening takes on a new dimension, as part of the everyday language of society.

By the same token, one can be critical of the theories above which invariably paint a picture in which we, as individuals, are duped by the self-help industry into being gullible users of and believers in what it provides. In this respect Giddens has a point when he argues that individuals have the capacity to be critical and reflective and so are well able to make up their own minds about what they get out of the self-help movement. And indeed, not all individuals choose to get involved, which implies that a certain level of healthy scepticism and pragmatism pervades individual choices when it comes to people's relationship with the self-help and happiness industry. Indeed, the topic of the next chapter – medicine in a risk society – reconceptualises the relations of late modernity and medicine in terms of scepticism, and resistance to medicine's assumed omnipotent medicalising pretensions.

References

Becker, G. and Rayo, L. (2007) 'Evolutionary efficiency and happiness', *Journal of Political Economy*, vol 115, no 2, pp 302–37.

Daniel, C. (1997) 'Staying sane', *New Statesman*, 3 October.

Dee, E. (2010) *Trends in Life Coaching – Reasons For Its Growing Popularity*, http://ezinearticles.com/?Trends-in-Life-Coaching---Reasons-For-Its-Growing-Popularity&id=3567958), January.

Department of Health (2007) *Trust, assurance and safety: The regulation of health professionals in the 21st century*, White Paper (www.dh.gov.uk/en/Publicationsandstatistics/Legislation/Regulatoryimpactassessment/DH_066044).

Dunoway, M.O. (2000) 'Assessing the potential of online psychotherapy', *Psychiatric Times,* vol 17, no 10, pp 1–9.

Ferguson, I. (2006) 'Neoliberalism, happiness and well-being', *Journal of International Socialism*, no 117 (www.isj.org.uk/?s=contents&issue=117).

Finn, D. (2000) 'From full employment to employability: a new deal for Britain's unemployed?', *International Journal of Manpower,* vol 21, no 5, pp 384–99.

Furedi, F. (2004) *Therapy culture: Cultivating vulnerability in an uncertain age*, London: Routledge.

Future Foundation (2004) *The age of therapy* (www.futurefoundation.net).

Giddens, A. (1991) *Modernity and self-identity: Self and society in the late modern age*, Cambridge: Polity Press.

Gunnell, B. (2004) 'The happiness industry', *New Statesman*, 6 September.

Holderman, L. (2007) 'Ozzy worked for those bleeping doors with the crosses on them: The Osbornes as social class narrative', in S. Redmond and S. Holmes (eds) *Stardom and celebrity: A reader*, London: Sage.

IFS (Institute for Fiscal Studies) (2009) Press release: 'Income inequality hit record high before the recession started' (www.ifs.org.uk/pr/hbai09.pdf).

Institute of Life Coaching (2003) *What is life coaching?* (www.lifecoachtraining. com).

Jeffries, S. (2008) 'Will this man make you happy?', *Guardian*, 24 June.

Jessop, B. (2006) *From Thatcherism to New Labour: Neo-liberalism, workfarism, and labour market regulation*, Department of Sociology, Lancaster University (www. comp.lancs.ac.uk/sociology/soc131rj.pdf).

Layard, R. (2005a) *Happiness: Lessons from a new science*, London: Allen Lane.

Layard, R. (2005b) 'Happiness is back', *Prospect*, no 108 (www.prospectmagazine. co.uk/2005/03/happinessisback/).

MacEacheran, M. (2004) *Stress sends Scots flocking to life coaches* (www.noble-manhattin.com).

Morrell, P. (2009) 'The trouble with therapy', *Therapy Today* (www.therapytoday. net/article/show/4/).

Odone, C. (1999) 'Counsellors have taught us to avoid sadness at all costs. But sometimes it's right to feel unhappy', *New Statesman*, 17 May.

Peck, J. and Theodore, N. (2000) Commentary: '"Work first": workfare and the regulation of contingent labour markets', *Cambridge Journal of Economics*, vol 24, pp 119–38.

Reginald, G. et al (2005) 'Road rage. Are our patients driving angry?', *Psychiatric Times*, vol 12, no 4, pp 1–8.

Rowe, D. (2000) 'Happy?', *The Observer*, 10 December (www.guardian.co.uk/ theobserver/2000/dec/10/life1.lifemagazine4).

Salerno, S. (2005) *SHAM. Self-help and actualisation movement: How the gurus of the self-help movement make us helpless*, London: Nicholas Brealey Publishing.

Thompson, J. (2005) 'Look what Carole Caplin and Cherie started: now 100,000 Britons have life coaches', *The Independent on Sunday*, 2 January.

FIVE

Medicine in a risk society: the forward march of medicalisation halted?

> The relationship between the scientific community and the general public has never been worse in living memory. (Haerlin and Parr, 1999)

> What is striking in the post-war years, during which new immunisations were introduced and uptake steadily increased, is that anti-vaccination campaigns, if they existed at all, had negligible influence. Even in the 1980s, when immunisation uptake increased rapidly – and when alternative health practices such as homeopathy began to gain in popularity – anti-vaccination ideas remained marginal. It was not until the late 1980s and early 1990s that anti-immunisation sentiment re-emerged and spread rapidly from a small number of people influenced by alternative health beliefs to find a much wider resonance in British society. The explanation for this phenomenon must be sought, not in the timeless appeal of superficially similar anti-immunisation arguments, but in the specific circumstances of modern Britain. (Fitzpatrick, 2004)

Introduction

It appears that public perceptions of science, and of medical science in particular, have been marked by a growing distrust in recent decades. The public relationship with medical science is Janus faced: on the one hand, science remains a pivotal source of knowledge about the world. On the other hand, medicine is also the subject of continual scrutiny and scepticism regarding its claims to cure without side effects. We seek the assistance and authority of science, while at the same time we appear to question the validity of its claims and worry over the objectivity of its findings, sometimes to the point where we are unsure about what to believe for the best in areas affecting our well-being.

In order to shed light on this dichotomy and highlight the practical value of social theory for understanding it, this chapter begins with an overview of 'risk society', a theoretical perspective on late modern society developed by Ulrich Beck (1992). The chapter then applies the concept of risk society to the controversies surrounding key immunisation campaigns, with a particular focus on the controversy surrounding the triple vaccine for measles, mumps and rubella (MMR). In particular, the chapter considers the recent controversy about the perceived safety of the MMR inoculation programme in the UK and applies the perspective of 'risk society' as a way of understanding the wider implications of this controversy for medical science in general. As with previous chapters, of particular relevance is how sociological concepts produce/represent the debate about the extent or otherwise of medicalisation in different ways that throw a different light on possible limits, opportunities and sources of resistance.

The wider aim of this chapter is to develop a critical understanding of risk society and how it applies to medical science. The chapter:

- examines the merits of the concept of risk society for understanding public reception of medical science;
- evaluates the extent and nature of this scepticism by drawing on the example of the MMR controversy and demonstrating how it strikes a chord with the core characteristics of what Beck defines as 'risk society';
- assesses the merits of the concept of risk society for understanding the contradictory location of medical science in modern society, with particular reference to the MMR controversy;
- concludes that the concept of risk society provides useful insights into the dilemmas facing medical science, yet also notes that risk consciousness is not homogenous, but highly variable according to social context and place.

The concept of 'risk society'

Since the early 1980s the word 'risk' and ideas relating to it have dominated public discourse. The traditional emphasis on the business of calculating and managing natural and societal risks in shipping and commerce has expanded to include much more of a concern with psychological approaches to perceptions of risk, with risk-averse communities and with how public and social policy is increasingly shaped by the concern with how to define risks and promote security. Much of the literature has worked under the unwritten assumption that risk is something external that is amenable to measurement and management across all areas of social life – by the insurance industries, by double-blind trials in medicine or by financial and economic models of the workings of money markets (Gabe et al, 1994). Sociology draws attention to how risks and the concept of risk are socially constructed in particular ways by different cultures, including academic communities. Individuals and groups experience 'cultural biases' towards perception of risk. Some express fatalism towards risk, others are more accepting of science's authority to know and manage risk, while other individuals and groups become oriented towards a strong sense of individualism and risk consciousness (Douglas and Wildavsky, 1982).

Above these present and localised intricacies, Beck's central theme of risk society argues that whole societies express a broad unity of shared ideas about the nature of 'risks which accords with their stage of development' (Beck, 1992). Beck argues that in late modernity a more general perception of risk is taking hold, one which feeds off a heightened sense of individualism and self-reflection on the dangers inherent in science and technology. He is not suggesting that the world is any more risky than it was in the past, when people (in industrial society) were perhaps even more exposed to natural disasters than they are today. What he is suggesting is that we now live in a more *risk-conscious society*. For Beck, risk consciousness has the following core features:

- There is a greater public awareness of the riskiness of aspects of life once considered mundane (from nuclear power to children playing in the streets).
- There is increasing uncertainty surrounding a whole range of personal and social risks, for example, about how pervasive or real or imagined they may be.
- People have a heightened sense of dependency upon professionals and scientists charged with managing risks, whether this is in medicine, the environment, or our daily welfare: for instance, the millions of hits per day on medical and health-related websites; the prevalence of expert-led public inquiries.
- There is a growing belief that risks are potentially unmanageable, which then fuels a growing scepticism among the public about the level of trust they ought to place in professionals, governments and scientists: for example, can we really trust what they have to say about 'mad cow disease' (bovine spongiform encephalopathy, or BSE), the spread of swine flu, or there really being no link between autism and the MMR inoculation?

These core features pool together and circulate throughout society, providing fertile ground for debating and contesting issues that were once thought to be relatively uncontroversial and where, broadly speaking, the science and knowledge was not in doubt. Beck argues that all this has changed in the late modern era. Recalling Giddens' argument discussed in previous chapters, that late modernity produces reflexive individuals more aware of the opportunities and constraints life presents to them, which makes society in turn more fluid and uncertain, Beck has a slightly different view of late modernity. For him, late modernity conjures up an uncertain relationship between the wider environment and the social world, premised on what is unknown and unintended as much as on what we think that we know and intend. Scientific knowledge – its claims about the world it seeks to know and control and its practical interventions – are, for Beck, reflexive in this latter sense. Reflexivity emerges in the growing awareness that science produces knowledge and intended results which harbour unknowns and unintended consequences. These two sides to science are not external to each other but inherent in science itself, making it an uncertain and risk-laden enterprise from beginning to end: we never know for certain whether what science knows and intends today will develop unknown, and so unintended, social consequences tomorrow. According to Beck's risk society thesis, individuals reveal a greater receptivity to these two sides to science, and so develop a greater sense of risk consciousness concerning the claims of science. This uncertainty also embraces medicine as a science, and patients and the parents of children who are patients of medicine.

Extending Beck's central premises to medicine, individuals in risk society expect more from science and medicine, but at the same time approach medicine in less deferential ways and with a heightened sensitivity to medicine as an unknown, risky enterprise. For example, we are now more inclined to debate the limits and negative consequences of orthodox medicine and to pose questions and discuss the credibility of alternative medicine (see Chapters Two and Three). We ask more searching questions about child welfare, whether children are adequately protected from abuse, for example, the recurrent debate about the dangers to children of being left unregulated or unattended to play in the street: can we any longer manage the risk to the community of 'the paedophile'? And, as we will go on to assess in more detail later, the public reveals an increasingly critical attitude to the 'goods' and 'bads' inherent in inoculation programmes such as MMR.

Why 'risk society'?

For Beck (1992), one reason for the emergence of the risk society is related to our increasing ability to communicate with each other, due, among other things, to the development of information technology (IT). We now have more knowledge circulating between government agencies, professional bodies, scientific communities and the public, and, moreover, this communication is global in nature. We are able to access information about medicine, health and well-being; about health threats and epidemics, both potential and real. This does not cause a greater sense of risk consciousness, but it does provide the means for it to develop and become integral to society. There is so much information from a variety of sources, so whom does one trust?

More fundamentally, the emergence of the risk society is related to our awareness of the threat posed by human action to the whole of society and the planet (Beck, 1992; 1999). Past societies did have plenty of real and terrifying risks to deal with, but in the past that risk was due to factors more external to humans and resulting from natural disaster. According to Beck, most of the major risks in the contemporary world result from human actions, not from nature. We once assumed that the advance of science and technology in all areas affecting human welfare would bring nature and society under control; we could master nature and increase our ability to manage the risks of nature and of society (unemployment, ill-health, destitution, and so on) at one and the same time, through using science and technology to increase our ability to create wealth and produce longer-living, healthier human beings.

This sense of security has been well and truly exposed to the insecurities of scientific practice, argues Beck, as technology and science applied to nature = nuclear catastrophe and environmental pollution; and technology and science applied to society = the social hazards related to, for example, a healthcare system based on biomedicine and its over-emphasis on drug technology, or a social welfare state that often sustains class exploitation and the oppressive status experienced by women in society. The risks now understood as inherent in the above make it clear to individuals, groups and states that they cannot actually manage risks as much as they once professed they could. Moreover, the growing impact of science and technology makes it increasingly difficult or impossible to manage the all-embracing risks that result from new discoveries or new inventions deemed to either make life better or advance our mastery over nature.

Therefore, 'risk society' is one in which the public is increasingly aware of the unmanageable, uncontrollable and omnipotent nature of environmental and social risks. Previous social divisions, based on the unequal distribution of wealth between rich and poor, are now joined by social inequalities of exposure to risks both potential and real. Risk society is a society in which the struggle to distribute risks from the rich to the poor is a major source of conflict (the recent hurricane Katrina in Atlanta, US, is a case in point, where environmental and social risks resulting from the devastation were borne overwhelmingly by the poorest and least powerful sections of society). Risk society is also a society in which the public demand more guidance from scientists and government agencies, at the very same time as they scrutinise those very same agencies and place in brackets their trust in them until they can reveal otherwise. However, in the face of public awareness that risks are increasingly outside government control, this merely adds to the public anxiety, mistrust and greater sense of risk consciousness concerning science.

Risk society and the state

Prior to the risk society, the state and governments organised themselves around the principle of a *safety state* in relation to the protection they claimed to offer the public with respect to natural and social hazards. Here, legitimacy rests on the ability of governments to regulate against the dangers inherent in industrial pollution and to secure the health and safety of the population. In risk society, the state and governments face a range of risks that are global in nature. Global warming is not something that one state can control, for example. It is likewise with the effects of nuclear disaster. Moreover, in a global economy with greater population mobility and interconnections between industries, the power of any one government to control the flow of potentially fatal viruses or infections, or local employment and welfare provision, becomes seriously weakened. In this sense the exposure to natural and social hazards is, from any one government's position, unmanageable. From a world characterised by 'positive sum games' (control nature and increase social safety) we have now entered a world of 'negative sum games' (scientific advance is problematic). This has produced a mindset of what one might describe as 'zero-tolerance' when it comes to questions of the role of government, professional bodies and science. We require their input even more now than we perhaps did when we used to take their input for granted. At the same time, we are not so trustful and are much more reflective and critical of their input. Meanwhile, government agencies and science itself become more aware of their own limitations, and so less willing to 'stick out their collective necks' when advising on issues of potential natural, social and medical hazards.

Beck has thus clearly developed an insightful thesis on late modernity, which has been taken up and developed by others in relation to health and medicine (Bunton et al, 1995; Petersen and Lupton, 1996; Gabe and Walklate, 2006). What light does Beck's account of risk society shed on the relationship between medicine, health and society? In particular, how does the concept of risk society represent the way we come to know medicalisation and its possible trajectories? Up until now the authority and power of medicine, institutionally and discursively, would seem to have grown in late modernity. However, on the face of it, Beck's risk society suggests a population more sceptical of science and medical science. Is this not evidence of the eclipse in the authority of medicine and so in the medicalisation of society? In risk society has medicalisation reached its limits? To address these related questions, the chapter develops insights from Beck towards an understanding of the role of medicine. The MMR controversy is discussed as a means of highlighting this role.

Medical panics: the case of MMR

On the one hand, medical science remains the touchstone for 'authoritative knowledge' and for deploying that knowledge in developing drugs and therapies that have proved to be both beneficial and also a source of control, stigma and alienation for those on the receiving end. On the other hand, medical science has been associated with panics and uncertainty regarding the pathology of infectious diseases or regarding its own role in the latter, as highlighted in the battle to discover any links between MMR and autism (or to assure people there is no link), against the potential global spread of bird flu and in fighting off a sudden acute respiratory syndrome (SARS) epidemic. The public reaction has been characterised by waves of panic and indifference. Take the SARS panic. The threat from SARS began in the autumn of 2002 when an atypical form of pneumonia was reported in a region of China followed in early 2003 by an outbreak among healthcare workers in Vietnam and then Hong Kong. In March 2003 the Director General of WHO declared the syndrome to be 'a worldwide health threat' so dangerous that the world's scientific and political communities must overcome competitive rivalries and work together to eradicate it (WHO, 2003). With the attention of the global media focused firmly on the SARS outbreak, in April 2003 the WHO initiated restrictions on travel to areas of China, Vietnam, Taiwan, Hong Kong and Canada as more cases of SARS were reported in these countries. Yet by May 2003 the threat and the rhetoric of impending global doom had been scaled back. Each of the infected countries reported a decrease in cases, and then no further outbreaks of SARS. The WHO lifted travel restrictions and the global media lost interest. SARS claimed 643 lives, and could certainly have claimed more, but for the coordinated response from the WHO.

Yet, as Lyons (2003) pointed out, the mass campaign, the panic-filled language used and the scope of the resources focused on SARS were out of proportion to the threat, once it was placed in perspective with other infectious diseases, such as malaria, which kills 3,000 children every day.

The same cycle of panic and indifference, of heightened states of scientific concern followed by apologetic withdrawal, is also evident in other cases, such as bird flu. The public grow increasingly fearful of contagion, sceptical of scientific advice, but increasingly anxious to secure more information, resulting in a spiral of fear and fascination which the media appears more than willing to endorse and manipulate. Science presents a confused image of itself to the public as conflicted, over-confident, unsure and equivocal over whether to treat events such as SARS and bird flu as social panics to be soothed or natural plagues to be screened and eradicated. Perhaps nowhere is this scepticism, fear and apparent indecision on the part of science more clearly evident than in the dispute concerning MMR inoculation.

In 1998, the leading medical journal *The Lancet* published a research paper by Dr Andrew Wakefield et al. Their study of 12 children suggested a possible link between the measles, mumps, and rubella (MMR) triple vaccination, bowel disease and the developmental disorder autism. The researchers were at pains to stress that they had not proved any causal connection between MMR and autism, but they claimed that the results of their study might be suggestive of an association, and that there ought to be further investigation to either confirm or reject any association. Subsequently, at a conference to discuss the findings, Dr Wakefield went on to argue more forcefully that the MMR vaccination might not be safe and that the government should perhaps at least consider separate programmes of inoculation for measles, mumps and rubella (Wakefield and Murch et al, 1998).

This research was met by a plethora of published research papers disputing the claims of a link with autism and emphasising the safety of the MMR vaccination. Fombonne (1998) reviewed registries of cases of inflammatory bowel disease and autism and failed to find an association; US scientists rejected the idea of a link between MMR and autism (Ashraf, 2001); and Bolton et al (2001) found no association between autism, measles and bowel disorder. One of the most comprehensive cohort studies, carried out in Denmark, found that, of the 537,303 children sampled, representing a population of 2,129,864 person-years, 440,655 (or 82.0%) had received the MMR vaccine. The sample contained 316 children with a diagnosis of autistic disorder and 422 with a diagnosis of other autistic-spectrum disorders. The researchers found that 'the relative risk of autistic disorder in the group of vaccinated children, as compared with the unvaccinated group, was 0.92 (95 percent confidence interval, 0.68 to 1.24), and the relative risk of another autistic-spectrum disorder was 0.83 (95 percent confidence interval, 0.65 to 1.07)'. And they concluded that their study 'provides strong evidence against the hypothesis that MMR vaccination causes autism' (Madsen et al, 2002). The National Autistic Society (2005) also went on record to declare that 'While we are aware that there are a number of parents who feel that their children's autism has been caused in this way, there is to the best of our knowledge no conclusive scientific evidence to prove this at present.'

Indeed, in their wide review of research studies concerning the possible links between MMR and autism, which incorporated research undertaken between 1998 and 2004, DeStefano and Thompson (2004, p 21) felt able to conclude that 'The evidence now is convincing that MMR vaccine does not cause autism...'. The graph in **Figure 5.1** appears to show that inoculation programmes have resulted in a decrease in the number of those contracting measles and a decline in the death rate for measles.

Figure 5.1: Measles notifications and deaths in England and Wales, 1940–2007

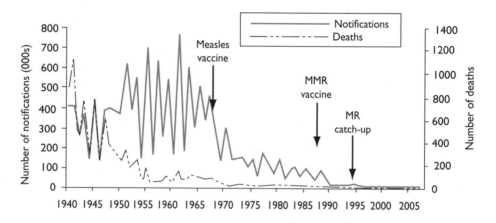

Source: Health Protection Agency (2008)

In summary, the welter of evidence contradicted the original claims about MMR. Medicine, to all intents and purposes, appeared to have justifiably won the argument, with the authority of medicine intact. Yet, despite the apparent weight of scientific evidence against the initial findings, and the apparent life-saving effect of inoculation programmes described in the graph, the public seemed to be unsure whom to believe, with a vocal minority rejecting the weight of scientific opinion – so much so that the UK government initiated a £3 million multi-media campaign across the country in an attempt to reassure the public that the MMR vaccine was safe and to counteract the fall-off in vaccinations, which was beginning to be a major cause for concern (*Lancet*, 2001). In spite of these interventions, across Britain, parents' uptake of MMR vaccination for their children fell. For example, it was estimated that in England and Wales rates fell to 84.1% in 2001–02, from the previous rate of 87.4% in 2000–01 (*Pharmaceutical Journal*, 2002). In Scotland, the rate of uptake fell from 95% achieved in the 1990s to just over 85% by 2001–02 (Scottish Office, 2002). After levelling off, immunisation rates had fallen back yet again by 2004–05, lower in England (81%) and Wales (82%) than in Scotland and Northern Ireland (88%) (National Statistics, 2006). As a result, the number of cases of measles has risen. For example, 'In 2006 and 2007 there were 1,726 confirmed cases in England and Wales – more than the previous 10 years put together', while it is 'estimated that around three million children aged 18 months to 18 years have missed either their first or second MMR vaccination' (Department of Health, 2008).

It appeared that, almost regardless of the weight of evidence and of government campaigns, the media and key consumer groups, as well as sections of the wider public, remained unconvinced by the scientists, or indeed by the government, of the safety of MMR in general and by the specific claim that MMR is not related to the onset of autism in young children. This scepticism has certainly been amplified in the media, where claims and counter-claims about the risks associated with MMR inoculation have featured ever since the claim of a supposed link was first made public. The following selection of newspaper headlines about MMR, from the many thousands of articles published between 1998 and 2005, indicates the tenor of the scare.

'Why my child won't have the MMR jab', *Guardian Unlimited*, 23 January 2001, Peter Todd.

'What is the truth behind MMR?', *Guardian Unlimited*, 5 December 2001, Linda Steele.

'Blair baby "has had" MMR jab', *The Observer*, 23 December 2001, Kamal Ahmed and Gaby Hinsliff.

'Baby taken to Paris for single jab', *Guardian*, 24 January 2001, Keith Perry.

'Tenfold increase in cases of autism alarms doctors', *Independent*, 5 April 2001.

'MMR vaccine is linked to bleeding disorder, says government adviser', *Independent*, 22 February 2001.

Given the intensity of media reporting of 'the MMR/autism scare', parents were perceived to be facing a dilemma: the choice appeared to be either to risk their children contracting measles, or else to expose them to the potential risk of autism or some other unknown malady. Some parents, mostly those who could afford to do so, decided to go for separate vaccinations; others decided against vaccination at all (hence the reductions in vaccination rates described above); others, who may have been sceptical, compelled by their desire to protect their children, were swayed by the authority of their GPs to accept the MMR jab.

Perhaps unsurprisingly, the media has often been portrayed as the principal agent in the MMR controversy. It is argued that the media was involved in loose reporting that fuelled the panic among a wider population, eager for more information, over the possible links between MMR and autism. Goldacre (2008) points out, for example, that 'less than a third of newspaper coverage in 2002 referred to the overwhelming evidence that MMR is safe, and only 11% mentioned that it is regarded as safe in the 90 other countries in which it is used' (Goldacre, 2008). Goldacre also points out that most of this coverage was undertaken by reporters who had no specific science training and so did not necessarily have the skills to interpret the evidence and instead gave equal status to the deliberations of scientists regardless of how the evidence was stacked up either confirming or rejecting the risk from MMR, so helping to sustain the idea that science was split over the issue of the safety of MMR (Goldacre, 2008).

The media clearly played a decisive role, but was it the principal causal factor? Others suggest not. As Bellaby reflects, 'The conduct of the media may have contributed to the miscommunication of risk, but it would be a mistake to suppose that the media led the public. Parents were predisposed to act in what seemed to them to be the interests of their children. The response of "the establishment" confirmed for some their suspicions that inconvenient truths would be covered up' (Bellaby, 2003, p 726).

Bellaby may have a point; the relationship between media and society is far more nuanced and individuals do not always receive information uncritically. Indeed, the media has been the topic of much sociological analysis (see, for example, Hall et al, 1980; Marris and Thornham, 1999; Curran and Gurevitch, 2005; and in relation to health, Seale, 2003). For our concerns, the principal points are that the media has a complex relation with society in which its own codes of meaning are subject to decoding, and so open to interpretation (Hall et al, 1980). We actively read, interpret and select information to form a knowledge base specific to our own life experiences, our age, gender, ethnicity and social class. In which case, young single adults may have a different perception of the risks associated with MMR than do parents; similarly with parents from different ethnic backgrounds, and so on. Moreover, specific social groups have the power to shape the media: government bodies, health professionals, parent groups, and so on. As Seale points out, seemingly 'routine media coverage of health-related topics' has often been 'linked with other moral and political agendas' (Seale, 2003, p 2). Such groups may have enough power to construct or deconstruct health panics surrounding events like the MMR/autism controversy. Therefore, perhaps rather than the media being the primary cause of the MMR panic, it is also in part responding to other social forces.

In this respect, it is worth noting the causal role of the anti-immunisation movement, which combines concerned parents and professionals critical of biomedicine with private sector interests. Here we perhaps have evidence of a collective voice against the imperatives of medicalisation as depicted in the previous two chapters. Perhaps the latter groups, in alliance with others such as those involved with the alternative health medicine movements, do provide a more sustainable basis of resistance against the seemingly unstoppable force of medicalisation – or perhaps not? The anti-immunisation movement includes groups such as Action Against Autism, Concerned Parents for Vaccine Safety, and

Global Vaccine Awareness League. The movement casts doubt on the medical impact of immunisations, laying emphasis on wider environmental causes, and claims that inoculations cause ill-health. Its global presence on established internet sites provides a counterpoint to official statements and claims emanating from scientific research, creating an aura of conspiracy and 'elevating parents' intuitive views about vaccines above science' (Gross, 2009). Yet, it is suggested that they too have links with private industry interests, particularly private health clinics promoting 'safer' vaccinations for those who can afford it, and legal aid networks with interests in pursuing court cases. In particular, Fitzpatrick (2004) has argued that sections of the legal establishment have played a vital role in inadvertently promoting the idea that there is an inherent risk between MMR and autism. For example, in 1994 the Legal Aid Board agreed to fund a number of claims for compensation for injury allegedly caused by MMR, the first case in which such funding had been used to finance scientific research. Over the intervening nine years to 2003, the Legal Aid Board (now Legal Services Commission) sponsored solicitors to the sum of £15 million in efforts to find some evidence to link MMR and autism. However, its research found no real links, although, according to Fitzpatrick, it did play a role in perpetuating the belief that there was a potential link, which the media and public then responded to by amplifying that belief.

Ultimately, the question of why the media and social groups have focused so much time and concern on the MMR controversy (as well as other related health interventions) is still to be resolved. The media has played a crucial role in creating panics. Along with vociferous social groups able to use the media as well as to be influenced by it, both are responding to events, not causing them. Is there a broader social basis to the fears and uncertainties generated by medical interventions such as MMR?

Fitzpatrick (2004) suggests that there is. He argues that 'the explanation for this phenomenon must be sought, not in the timeless appeal of superficially similar anti-immunisation arguments, but in the specific circumstances of modern Britain'. Fitzpatrick is perhaps unduly critical of the impact of the latter. However, he does identify three social factors underpinning the specific circumstances of late modern Britain. Firstly, he identifies the dominating market ideology of the 1980s and 1990s, which infused public consciousness as well as public policy with promises of empowerment of the individual consumer with rights and responsibilities – including the rights to buy their own home, choose private healthcare and shop around for the best schools for their children, and responsibilities to look after their own health and be economically independent. Secondly, he identifies the lack of direct experience of the effects of infectious disease among the present generation of parents, *due to the success of immunisation programmes*, which has had an adverse effect on their ability to make informed judgements, based on experience of the relative benefits of immunisation as against the minor risks associated with immunisation. Thirdly, and partly as a consequence of the two preceding factors, Fitzpatrick argues that health interventions have become increasingly *politicised*, the subject of 'intense personal discussion (tending to involve fathers as well as mothers) and subject to wider public and political influences. Decisions about MMR tended to reflect attitudes on a range of issues raised by the controversy: 'the authority of medical science and the medical profession, the trustworthiness of vaccine manufacturers, civil servants and politicians' (Fitzpatrick, 2004). According to Fitzpatrick, all three factors – consumerism coupled with the right to choose, lack of direct experience of measles outbreaks and the generally politicised nature of everyday healthcare – combine to create a highly critical audience for the media.

Fitzpatrick's argument invokes a world of uncertainty and individualisation; a world very similar to that painted by Beck, and which, Beck (1992) suggests, is becoming increasingly risk conscious and risk averse. We are, argues Beck, living in the presence of a 'risk society'. In 'risk society', suggests Beck, we become more aware of the risks that humans manufacture and more aware of structural inequalities in the distribution of risks between social groups. What scope does Beck's concept of risk society provide us with for contextualising the MMR controversy? The next section draws on Beck's thesis to demonstrate this broader understanding of the MMR panic. It does so in order to raise the more general question as to why, in recent decades, the public scrutiny of science and medicine and the level of scepticism towards it have reached new heights, and where this leaves the process of medicalisation.

'Risk society' and MMR

To what extent can the concept of risk society help to illuminate the MMR debate? It was mentioned earlier that one of the core characteristics of risk society is a greater public awareness of the riskiness of aspects of life that were once considered mundane. In this respect, MMR inoculation was an accepted medical intervention for 10 years, only to then be suddenly perceived as a major risk to health, on the basis of a small-scale research paper that was quickly debunked. Likewise the increasing uncertainty surrounding medical and health-related risks – for example, about how pervasive or real they are – becomes manifest in the media reporting of MMR, which tends to be undertaken in cycles, each one having its own intensity. But in all the reporting there are always arguments for and against the threat which leave the issue open to immense doubt, and so to fear and uncertainty, even though more generally one can see that recent debates concerning bird flu, BSE and MMR reveal a heightened sense of dependency upon professionals and scientists charged with managing risks (a major feature of the fear and fascination ascribed to MMR inoculation programmes and their imputed but never-proved connection with autism). It would appear that, as suggested by the risk society thesis, the more questioning parents are about MMR, the more dependent they become on the last word of the latest science report, only for this too to be treated with scepticism. There is also a growing belief that risks are potentially unmanageable, with the resulting growing scepticism among the public concerning the level of trust they ought to place in professionals, governments and scientists: can we really trust what they have to say about 'mad cow disease', or about what they pronounce regarding the links between autism and MMR?

More generally, Beck's concept of 'risk society' has had a major influence on health research, directly and indirectly, across the social sciences (Gabe et al, 1994; Bunton et al, 1995; Lupton, 1995; Gabe and Walklate, 2006; Taylor-Gooby and Zinn, 2006)). In recent years the concept has helped to illuminate individual experiences of risks associated with medical interventions with the broader social context of a risk-conscious society. One recent study in this area found that personal narratives of family health history, birth, illnesses and other events with respect to decisions over whether their child should have the MMR vaccine are framed by the 'personalisation of responsibility in the "risk society" ... where distrusting the capacity of public institutions to manage technological risks, parents feel they have no one to blame but themselves' (Poltorak et al, 2005, p 717).

Other research influenced by Beck points out how risk consciousness pervades public information about MMR. Risk management is now a central part of the healthcare industry, monitoring and surveillance of procedures, health complications and costs of litigation (Gabe et al, 1994, p 2). Moreover, government too appears to be in the thrall of 'risk consciousness': with respect to MMR, government pamphlets setting out the case for vaccination tend to ignore arguments concerned with the wider social utility gained from herd immunity and instead adopt the perspective of risk by attempting on the one hand to persuade parents of the low risk of vaccination and high risks of not vaccinating their child, while on the other hand explaining how non-compliance is irrational (Poltorak et al, 2005). The stance taken by official and professional sources of knowledge is increasingly one dictated by eliminating as much as possible their own exposure to risk of getting it wrong in the eyes of the public. Hence 'open government' is as much about auditing levels of risks and letting the public decide as it is about guidance, transparency and partnership. At the same time, and as discussed earlier, parents who are faced with making a choice to have their child inoculated and with the burgeoning quantity of information at their disposal are exposed to a greater sense of risk of making the 'wrong' decision on behalf of their child: Beck's argument that current evidence of the good of science may be no guarantee against its becoming 'bad' science in the future, in the light of experience.

Is it possible, then, that this may be evidence of a challenge to the onward march of medicalisation? In one respect, the attention paid to reflexive individuals and parents who challenge the authority of medicine over MMR links to autism suggests this may be the case. The movement against inoculation was a challenge to medical orthodoxy and to the perceived links between it and the state, as they jointly closed ranks to push through triple inoculations. However, in a risk society one might also expect critical, reflexive and risk-averse individuals to be inclined to seek security and certainty of prognosis in order to manage the range of multiple health risks they and their relatives face. In this context, medicine is useful in providing individuals with the certainty of medical labels to clarify behaviours that they find difficult to comprehend, such as the parent seeking the security of the label 'hyperactivity disorder' for their child, or the adult accepting the label 'manic depressive'. On the one hand, one could argue that a risk society is fertile ground for the authority of medicine to be challenged by alternative medicines, as health consumers shop around (as some parents did in relation to single vaccines for mumps, measles and rubella) and so manage the perceived risks involved in the near-monopoly of power over provision exerted by orthodox medicine. On the other hand, however, 'risk consciousness' and 'risk aversion' related to medical science are perhaps just as likely to facilitate the growth of a pervasive 'health consciousness' among a critically reflexive population. Anti-immunisation movements are just as preoccupied with health issues as those groups that promote alternative medicine. One could argue that for both groups the intense focus on health and medicine means that everyday activities are judged by worries about what they add to or detract from one's health, rather than enjoyed for their own sake. This is just as much part of the process of medicalisation.

Indeed, closer inspection of the MMR controversy reveals not so much challenge but insecurity and collective stasis among anti-immunisers concerning alternatives. The fall in the number of MMR vaccinations is not met by any wider resistance to medicine itself; it was more a case of voting with one's feet and hoping this would generate more awareness *within medicine* itself with regard to a thorough investigation into MMR. It could just as easily be argued that being exposed to a variety of potential risks and being more reflexive of such information makes individuals more vulnerable, not necessarily more empowered to check the onward march of medicalisation. The latter invokes Illich's argument concerning the cultural passivity of medicalisation in his discussion of the impact of cultural iatrogenesis, raised in Chapter Two.

We observe the potentially disempowering logic of risk consciousness more clearly at a more general level, particularly where the concept of risk has refocused attention on public health programmes. By emphasising *populations* rather than at-risk *individuals*, one argument is that risk becomes a means of governing whole populations (Petersen and Lupton, 1996) through the provision of medical advice that slips easily into moral guidance on how to conduct oneself in public; through, for example, healthy eating targets, fitness regimes and other behaviour modifications. These forms of advice provide a means through which to govern populations, marking out the deviant from the compliant, the normal from the abnormal (Petersen, 1997). Indeed, public health programmes focused on abstract statistical trends do not so much target those who have an illness or who happen to be in need of health intervention in the *present*, as target the entire population by estimating and measuring who may be at risk in the *future*. This general shift towards a future orientation, marking out potential risks that may or may not transpire, is further fertile ground for medical panics in the present, such as the MMR controversy on which this chapter has focused. If government and medicine place such importance on medical interventions oriented towards attempting to measure future health risks, this in itself feeds uncertainty in the population (not to mention the media) about the validity or otherwise of such indicators.

Moreover, while the MMR/autism debate can be explained within the theoretical framework of an emerging risk society, others have argued that the concept of risk society is itself too general and abstract and thus glosses over as much as it reveals about social reactions to health interventions and medical science such as the MMR controversy. One criticism is that Beck's conceptualisation appears to assume that we all operate with the same definition and understanding of 'risk', regardless of culture. Yet, as Douglas (1970) argued, one person's perspective on what is and isn't 'risky' will be different from that of another person brought up in a different family background or wider culture. For example, in one neighbourhood the norm may be that children play freely in the streets; in others the norm may be for children to play in a more controlled manner, in 'safe areas' and at specific times. Both situations imply different perceptions of risk, so this weakens any argument about an all-embracing 'risk consciousness'. Experiences of risk also change over the life course of the same individual: what one may have considered risk free in one's teens may now be considered gravely risky with respect to one's own children.

Taking this recognition of cultural differences further, we could argue that the perceived risks associated with MMR and autism will differ substantially within society, with some not viewing any serious risk, others arguing that there is a serious risk, and variations in between. Indeed, the ability to pay for alternative treatments, for example separate measles, mumps and rubella vaccinations, may be another factor in how one experiences exposure to 'risk': ironically, if one has money, and so the choice, then the risk in many ways becomes an issue, although one which you perhaps feel able to resolve through the purchase of separate injections of measles, mumps and rubella (Fitzpatrick, 2004). On the other hand, for those who cannot afford to pay and who are faced with restricted market choice, their sense of risk and anxiety may not be of the same scale because (1) they cannot do that much about it and (2) other material issues may be more important to them, such as securing and maintaining employment and keeping a home together.

Risk, in other words, 'is not randomly distributed', 'we are not all', as Furedi observes, 'equally at risk from social and natural environmental factors' (Furedi, 2002). We know that children from working-class backgrounds are far more likely to be injured or to die from a car accident than are children from middle-class backgrounds. Being unemployed, with all the associated negative social consequences (which affect the lower classes much more than any other class) makes one much more likely to be at risk of heart disease, stress-related illnesses, suicide, and so on. In sum, it is argued that there tends not to be any recognition of these *class-based mal-distributions* of risk in Beck's account of 'risk society'. This can be explained partly by his argument that 'risk society' is a new stage in society, and therefore a shift from the 'old' patterns of social inequalities based on class situation. Beck is not, of course, arguing that class inequalities no longer exist, but he is arguing that they are not the principle around which society pivots (Franklin, 2006). Yet, as we have just intimated, the more one draws the focus back to traditional forms of social inequality – not only social class, but also gender, ethnicity and age – the more Beck's claims about a 'new society' based on 'risk' must factor in the social and cultural context that gives meaning to our understanding and experience of risk (Uwe Engel and Strasser, 1998).

Moreover, many of the same processes that Beck identifies as fundamental to the shift towards 'risk society' – changes in the welfare state and patterns of employment – can also be understood as the consequences of the capitalist class achieving greater social control over the working class through the reduction of trade union power and through the threat of poverty, unemployment and insecure employment, resulting from the expansion of the market and the profit motive into more areas of social life, including social welfare and health. We noted in Chapter Two that this expansion of the market can be understood as a struggle over the commodification of key goods and services (including medical interventions), which become 'fictitious capital', a term highlighting their contradictory nature as useful objects of social and personal need and a source of monetary value for sale and purchase (Polanyi, 1957).

Social class inequalities aside, Beck's concept of risk society would also appear to conflate two separate issues: the progress that science makes in advancing discoveries, and how those discoveries are then used within society. Beck tends to conflate the two when developing his critique of science, technology and risk. Einstein's theory of relativity was one discovery among others that helped to pave the way for splitting the atom and developing nuclear power, which was then used to create nuclear weapons of mass destruction. Does this make Einstein's endeavour a case of manufactured risks and 'bad' rather than 'good' science, inasmuch as it is *inherently hazardous*? Or can we separate the science from the use we make of it? Beck's conflation makes it possible to take his argument and turn it into an anti-science manifesto.

As Furedi (2002) points out, the conflation of risk with anti-science is conducive to a society in which change and the future are experienced as a negative risk instead of an opportunity for the advancement of human well-being. Furedi (2002) suggests that anti-science, coupled with the prevalence of risk consciousness, leads to greater constraints on individual freedom of choice, despite the rhetoric of individualism in consumer society. He explains that individuals today are pressured into being responsible for the health and welfare of themselves and their immediate families. The level of public involvement of individuals has been weakened by the need to look after one's own self-interest – a need enforced by an increasingly uncertain labour market and contracts of employment, alongside the growth of a consumerist society and notions of the privatised consumer (set further adrift, for example, from the people who produce the products they purchase). In such an environment we feel more alone within society and view society as a number of potential threats against which we must be vigilant. The main beneficiaries of this situation, argues Furedi (2004), are the professional consumer groups who step into the fray apparently to represent the interests of individuals in society. His claim is that they are more often unelected bodies who merely represent their own interests. A number of loosely associated non-governmental groups covering diverse issues in alternative health and medicine, consumer and food groups, fill the political void left by those privatised individuals mentioned above and become the key players in the debate about MMR.

Conclusion

This chapter began with the observation that contemporary society's relationship with medical science is Janus faced. On the one hand, science remains a pivotal source of knowledge about the world, while, on the other hand, it is also the subject of continual scrutiny and scepticism regarding its claims. We seek the assistance and authority of science, while at the same time we appear to question the validity of its claims and worry over the objectivity of its findings, sometimes to the point where we are unsure about what to believe for the best in areas affecting our well-being. Taking up Fitzpatrick's words at the beginning of this chapter, that 'the explanation for this phenomenon must be sought, not in the timeless appeal of superficially similar anti-immunisation arguments, but in the specific circumstances of modern Britain', the aim of this chapter has been to examine the merits of the concept of risk society for an understanding of the contradictory location of medical science in modern society, with particular reference to the MMR controversy.

It has been shown that although the concept of risk society covers a vast range of social issues, it can help to illuminate the role of medical science and its relation to society, as articulated through the discussion of MMR. The MMR controversy, as argued, strikes a chord with the core characteristics of risk society mentioned earlier, enabling one to place it in a wider social context that deepens our understanding of its wider significance and relation to other medical anxieties in a period of social change. However, the extent to which risk society presents a challenge to the onward march of medicalisation is debatable. As argued earlier, in one respect the attention paid to reflexive individuals and parents challenging the authority of medicine over MMR and its links to autism suggests that this may be the case. However, closer inspection reveals not so much a challenge as insecurity and collective stasis about alternatives.

The chapter has also pointed out that Beck's conceptualisation of risk society may tend to be too general and insufficiently sensitive to the cultural context within which experiences of risk unfold. The more we consider the latter, the more aware we become that risk consciousness is highly variable and dependent on social context and place. The concept marginalises social class conflict and inequalities, which arguably remain pivotal to how we experience risks and are able to deal with them. Risk society also tends to paint too bleak a picture of science and technological changes as inherently dangerous, rather than as sources of social progress and advancement. While perhaps not intended, this offers fertile ground for anti-enlightenment sentiment, which tends to subsume all knowledge into relations of power. These criticisms do not negate the explanatory power of 'risk society' so much as point towards a more complex way of understanding how the experience of 'risk' is more open ended and embedded within more enduring social inequalities and conflicts within capitalist society.

Questions for further reflection

1 Define the concept of 'risk society'.
2 Search the news media for three instances in which medical authority is being challenged and assess the merits of Beck's 'risk society' for arriving at an understanding of this challenge.
3 Explain how risk society might be useful to understand 'therapy culture'. Outline the benefits and limitations of Beck's concept of 'risk society'.

References

Ashraf, H. (2001) 'US expert group rejects link between MMR and autism', *The Lancet,* vol 357, p 1341.

Beck, U. (1992) *Risk society. Towards a new modernity*, London: Sage Publications.

Beck, U. (1999) *World risk society*, Cambridge: Polity Press.

Bellaby, P. (2003) 'Communication and miscommunication of risk: understanding UK parents' attitudes to combined MMR vaccination', *British Medical Journal,* vol 327, pp 725–8.

Bolton, P.F. et al (2001) 'Association between idiopathic infantile macrocephaly and autism spectrum disorders', *The Lancet*, vol 358, pp 726–7.

Bunton, R., Burrows, R. and Nettleton, S. (1995) *The sociology of health promotion: Critical analyses of consumption, lifestyle and risk*, London: Routledge.

Curran, J. and Gurevitch, M. (eds) (2005) *Mass media and society* (4th edn), London: Hodder Education.

Department of Health (2008) 'National MMR vaccine catch-up campaign launched' (www.dh.gov.uk/en/News/Recentstories/DH_086861).

DeStefano, F. and Thompson, W.W. (Feb 2004) 'MMR vaccine and autism: an update of the scientific evidence', *Expert Review of Vaccines*, vol 3, no 1, pp 19–22.

Douglas, M. (1970) *Purity and danger: An analysis of concepts of pollution and taboo*, London, Routledge.

Douglas, M. and Wildavsky, A. (1982) *Risk and culture*, Berkeley, CA: University of California Press.

Fitzpatrick, M. (2004) 'MMR, risk, choice, chance, *British Medical Bulletin*, vol 69, no 1, pp 143-53.

Fombonne E. (1998) 'Inflammatory bowel disease and autism', *The Lancet*, vol 351, no 9107, p 955.

Franklin, J. (2006) 'Politics and risk', in M. Gabe and S. Walklate (eds) *Beyond the risk society: Critical reflections on risk and security*, Maidenhead: Open University Press.

Furedi, F. (2002) *Culture of fear: Risk-taking and the morality of low expectations*, London: Continuum International Publishing Group.

Furedi, F. (2004) *Therapy culture: Cultivating vulnerability in an uncertain age*, London: Routledge.

Gabe, M. and Walklate, S. (eds) (2006) *Beyond the risk society: Critical reflections on risk and security*, Maidenhead: Open University Press.

Gabe, J., Kelleher, D. and Williams, G. (1994) *Challenging medicine*, London: Routledge.

Goldacre, B. (2008) 'The media's MMR hoax', *Guardian*, 30 August.

Gross (2009) 'A broken trust: lessons from the vaccine–autism wars', *Plos Biology*, May (www.plosbiology.org/home.action;jsessionid=6036C6C39E1475284D 71FC5CF87E3914).

Hall, S. et al (1980) *Culture, media, language*, London: Hutchinson.

Haerlin, B. and Parr, D. (1999) *Nature*, vol 400, 5 August, p 499.

Health Protection Agency (2008) (www.hpa.org.uk/web/HPAweb&HPAwebStandard/ HPAweb_C/1195733756107).

Lancet (2001) 'UK starts campaign to reassure parents about MMR-vaccine safety', vol 357, p 290.

Lupton, D. (1995) *The imperative of health: Public health and the regulated body*, London: Sage.

Lyons, R. (2003) 'Who's to blame for the SARS panic?', May (www.spiked-online. com/Printable/00000006DDA8.htm).

Madsen, K.M. et al (2002) 'A population-based study of measles, mumps, and rubella vaccination and autism', *The New England Journal of Medicine*, vol 347, no 19 (http://content.nejm.org/cgi/content/short/347/19/1477).

Marris, P. and Thornham, S. (1999) *Media studies: A reader*, Edinburgh: Edinburgh University Press.

National Autistic Society (2005) 'Is there a link between MMR and autism?', January (www.nas.org.uk/nas/jsp/polopoly.jsp?d=108&a=3343).

National Statistics (2006) 'Focus on health' (www.statistics.gov.uk/cci/nugget. asp?id=1334).

Petersen, A. (1997) 'Risk, governance and the new public health', in A. Petersen and R. Bunton, *Foucault, health and medicine*, London: Routledge.

Petersen, A. and Lupton, D. (1996) *The new public health: health and self in the age of risk*, London and Thousand Oaks, CA: Sage.

Pharmaceutical Journal (2002) 'MMR uptake shows small recovery', vol 269, no 7217, p 428 (www.pharmj.com/news/2002/10oct/20021003_mmr.html).

Polanyi, K. (1957 [1944]) *The great transformation: The political and economic origins of our time*, Boston: Beacon Press by arrangement with Rinehart & Company Inc..

Poltorak, M., Leach, M., Fairhead, J. and Cassell, J. (2005) '"MMR talk" and vaccination choices: an ethnographic study in Brighton', *Social Science & Medicine*, vol 61, no 3, pp 709–19.

Seale, C. (2003) *Media and health*, London: Sage.

Scottish Office (2002) 'Small rise in uptake' (www.scotland.gov.uk/News/ Releases/2002/06/1729).

Taylor-Gooby, P. and Zinn, J.O. (2006) *Risk in social science*, Oxford: Oxford University Press.

Uwe Engel, U. and Strasser, H. (1998) 'Global risks and social inequality: critical remarks on the risk-society hypothesis', *The Canadian Journal of Sociology / Cahiers canadiens de sociologie*, vol 23, no 1, pp 91–103.

Wakefield, D. and Murch, S. et al (1998) 'Ileal-lymphoid-nodular hyperplasia, non-specific colitis, and pervasive development disorder in children', *The Lancet*, vol 351, pp 637–41.

WHO (World Health Organization) (2003) Press release, 'Severe acute respiratory syndrome (SARS) spreads worldwide' (www.who.int).

SIX

Moral panics and medicalisation: the case of binge drinking

Societies appear to be subject, every now and then to periods of moral panic. Conditions, episodes, person or groups of persons emerge to become defined as a threat to societal values and interests. (Cohen, 2002, p 9)

Teenagers are gripped by an 'epidemic' of binge-drinking, so severe it has seen consumption of alcohol almost double in the past decade. (Halle, 2002)

The doctors, the ministers and the police may see it as an argument about violent crime, facial scars and anti-social behaviours. But for Britain's binge drinkers themselves it's not about any of this. It's about a spanking good night out, and nothing else. (Raynor, 2004)

Introduction

A concept closely related to risk society is 'moral panic'. The concept describes the process whereby society is periodically gripped by a panic over the perceived moral threat posed by events or actions of one or more social groups. From the vantage point of risk society and late modernity, which argues that society is in a state of permanent flux and transition, exhibiting rising insecurities and populated by more critical-reflexive individuals, one might expect moral panics to occur with increased regularity. It is argued later that this would seem to be the case. This chapter addresses the extent to which moral panics serve as another medium through which the medicalisation of social problems that have their origin in wider social structures manifests. The scope of medicalisation focused on here invokes the distinction raised by C.R. Wright Mills (1959) between personal troubles and public issues. Mills argued that individuals experience problems and challenges that they can influence and change, and which they and others feel responsible for resolving. He defined these as personal troubles. More often, though, the problems and challenges facing individuals are public issues originating in larger social institutions and structures which individuals have little power to control and are only resolvable through wider social changes. This chapter discusses how moral panics act as the medium for obscuring social issues by transforming them into personal troubles.

The chapter uses the example of moral panics over binge-drinking youth to address the tensions and contradictions inherent in this mediation. Binge drinking has remained a popular topic of discussion and hyperbole in the mass media. During the 2000s news media coverage portraying negative images of anti-social, binge-drinking youth has never been far from the public eye. The tabloid press led the way with lurid stories about escalating incidents of binge drinking, which is now seen as the new 'British disease'. The UK government and the British Medical Association have also expressed their growing concern over an epidemic of binge drinking, among youth in particular.

The chapter first provides an overview of the concept of moral panic. It then describes how binge drinking has become a public cause for concern. Here we explain the way in which binge drinking is defined as a social problem. Drawing on evidence from the media, health professionals and government sources, we will consider how each of these sources treats binge drinking as something objective, out of control and to be either cured or controlled. The chapter then examines the concept of moral panic as a way of approaching binge drinking from a different angle, one that does not assume that it is an objective fact, but a constructed stigma. Here, the emphasis shifts to examining for whom drinking is a social problem, who is defining binge drinking and what interests are served by such definitions. The concept of moral panic is used, in particular, to explore the relationship between the attention focused on binge-drinking youth and wider sources of social change and uncertainty that immediately affect young people today. Here we consider the connection between society's conception of youth as a social problem and society's difficulties in guaranteeing employment and social advancement, which is to say a future, for youth. The chapter concludes that moral panics about binge-drinking youth serve to medicalise wider social concerns about the place of youth in society. The chapter:

- outlines the concept of moral panic;
- describes the extent of binge drinking and the way binge drinking is defined as both a health and a social problem through the media, government and the medical profession;
- evaluates the concept of moral panic as a way of approaching binge drinking as a social construction;
- considers the connection between society's conception of youth as a social problem and society's difficulties in guaranteeing employment and social advancement.

The concept of 'moral panic'

Moral panic first became popularised with Stanley Cohen's study of youth culture in the 1960s (Cohen, 2002) and has underpinned a mass of research ever since. As Goode and Ben-Yehuda reflect in the preface to the second edition of their book (2009, p x), 'an almost literal ton of books, articles and chapters has been written on the moral panic, on topics as diverse as crime, child molestation and priestly paedophilia, extraterrestrials, terrorism, flag desecration, illegal aliens, crack cocaine, designer drugs, ecstasy, raves, video "nasties", gangsta–rap, horror comics, alien abductions, the red scare, the white slave traffic, conspiracies, satanic ritual abuse and murder in day care centres'.

The concept has its intellectual origins in the wider social interactionist approach within sociology. This approach views knowledge, actions, meanings and ways of understanding as originating in and through the web of everyday individual interactions that we weave. Accordingly, individuals come to share meaning about what is right and wrong, proper and improper behaviour, normal or deviant behaviour, and so on. However, rather than seeing deviancy as intrinsic to the individual or social group, the concept of moral panic draws on a more reflexive appreciation within interactionism of the role of powerful groups in defining what is 'normal', or which groups or individuals are 'deviant'. In this sense, Cohen's theory of moral panic is part of a more reflexive appreciation of how deviancy can be constructed in different ways and is a resource of the powerful inasmuch as it seeks to address questions such as who benefits and who loses from the classification of some behaviours as 'deviant' or 'normal'. Cohen's application of the concept of moral panic is therefore part of what he refers to as 'a skeptical revolution' within the social interactionist perspective in general and the sociology of deviance in particular (Cohen, 2002, p 3).

Turning to the technicalities of moral panic, Cohen observed how the media, government and a range of professional and public institutions periodically focused on the actions of social groups and individuals as a threat to the social order or what they took to be the prevailing moral consensus. In this respect, Cohen observed how societies every now and then appear to be subjected

> to periods of moral panic. A condition, episode, person or group of persons emerges to become defined as a threat to societal values and interest; its nature is presented in a stylised and stereotypical fashion by the mass media; the moral barricades are manned by editors, bishops, politicians and other right-thinking people; socially accredited experts pronounce their diagnoses and solutions; ways of coping are evolved or (more often) resorted to; the condition disappears, submerges or deteriorates and becomes more visible. Sometimes the object of panic is quite novel and at other times it is something which has been in existence long enough, but suddenly appears in the limelight. Sometimes the panic passes over and is forgotten, except in folklore and collective memory; at other times it has more serious and long-lasting repercussions and might produce such changes as those in legal and social policy or even in the way the society conceives itself. (Cohen, 2002, p 9)

Cohen explains that moral panics help to reinforce established values in periods of acute social anxiety. They are a means of maintaining social control by invoking modern-day 'folk devils' to galvanise a moral consensus towards strengthening the law against 'social deviants'. His early work has been extended by Hall's (1978) research into the fear and fascination with 'muggings' in the 1970s, which emphasised the ideological role of official agencies working to shape and develop the moral panic over 'rising incidents' of mugging against the wider backdrop of economic recession and wider social conflict. Thompson (1998) revised the theory of moral panic by arguing that moral panics are now ever-present processes in contemporary society, often overlapping each other. Whereas for Cohen moral panics were episodic, exceptions to the rule of established norms, for Thompson moral panics have become the rule: society is engulfed in wave after wave of moral panics, about the AIDS epidemic, bird flu, asylum-seekers 'swamping' the country, English football hooliganism, obesity, child abuse, stranger danger, anti-social youth behaviour, and so on, to the latest moral panics surrounding 'binge-drinking youth' – out of control and a danger to themselves and law-abiding citizens who can 'drink responsibly'. In what follows we consider Cohen's conceptual understanding and then draw on Hall's identification of the wider ideological and structural functions played by the moral panic in relation to binge drinking.

Cohen (2002) suggested that there was a distinct developmental logic to the creation of moral panics, focused around a contemporary 'folk devil' which he defined as a process of 'deviance amplification'. Deviance amplification is seen more or less as a spiral, as shown in **Figure 6.1**.

Figure 6.1: A model of the social spiral of a moral panic

The initial behaviour is labelled 'deviant' by specific claim makers (whether they happen to be the media, official agencies or professional bodies);

Information is relayed from primary definers to the media, and thence to the wider society;

There is a negative social reaction;

The deviant groups become isolated and react by resisting the consensus view and possibly becoming more actively deviant;

The increased 'deviance' leads to increased social control, leading to the clamour for legal crackdowns or tighter regulations, depending on the specifics of the moral panic and the nature of the deviant group;

At this point the whole spiral escalates further, subsides, or starts all over again.

A moral panic does not equate to the claim that the focus of the panic is invented; the issues do exist. Rather, the claim is that the *manner* in which issues are constructed is grossly exaggerated and *blown out of proportion* as a *national threat*, on a scale never before witnessed.

Cohen was also at pains to stress that the driving force of a moral panic lay in the *wider context of society*, and in particular with 'an ensuing climate of cultural ambiguity'(Hier, 2003, p 6). The initial site or focus for the panic was not the most vital issue, rather it was a manifestation of a much wider concern; our wider anxiety over broader societal changes. The real panic is over a threat or perceived threat to fundamental rules and norms of society; a threat to social consensus. Where once society at least enjoyed the perception of having definable rules and norms, shared and understood by the majority, these rules and norms are now called into question and have become corroded from within. The moral panic is a means of giving tangible expression to and resisting wider transformations of the social order, but is often less understood.

We see this historically, when panics about youths drinking to excess have arisen when a society is under increasing strain or is in the process of major economic change and social upheaval. In the case of Holland in the 17th century, a panic over unruly, out-of-control, drunken youth was inflamed by a combination of natural disasters, economic setbacks and war, all of which were deemed to be a sign of God's wrath. The reaction or panic acted as a medium through which moral and social order based on the work ethic and sobriety could find expression.

As the following quote suggests, the fear and fascination accorded to alcohol abuse has a long history:

> During the 1650s and 1660s, the Dutch Republic witnessed a wave of moral panic created by moralists. Every natural disaster, economic setback, and war that the Republic was involved in was considered to be a sign of God's wrath on Holland's newly acquired freedom, wealth, and secular society. Much of the finger pointing was directed toward Holland's young people, who were accused of being vain, defying the Sabbath, and visiting the theatre, gambling, drinking, and fornicating. (Roberts and Groenendijik, 2005, p 327)

Here the escapades of Holland's youth provided tangible expression of the nation's economic setbacks and the erosion of religious influence within the new republic.

Drink also became a national issue of concern in the 18th century and the 'second hundred years war' between Britain and France (the struggle to establish geographical boundaries of capitalist development and capital accumulation), and then during the Industrial Revolution, providing tangible expression of the wider issue of labour discipline and the threat this posed to industrial profits. As Hunt reflects,

> Fear over the effects of excessive drinking is woven into our cultural
> fabric. In the 18th century the great moral panic was gin. In 1742 a
> population barely a tenth the size of today's consumed 19m gallons
> of gin – 10 times as much as is drunk today. In centuries to come
> 'Saint Monday', the custom of taking off the first day of each week
> to recover from weekend excesses, proved an essential component of
> agricultural life … [The] forerunners of today's Coronet super-pubs,
> gin palaces resembled factory assembly lines with an equally industrial
> attitude to drinking. There was little furniture and no food, just a long
> bar surrounded by gin barrels – encouraging a quick and furious
> consumption of alcohol. (Hunt, 2004)

During the First World War the UK government became concerned that alcohol
consumption might adversely affect the war effort and in 1915 it took steps to
alter opening hours and the strength of alcohol. By 1918 opening hours had
been dramatically reduced, leading the way to the Licensing Act of 1921, which
established weekday and weekend opening hours that remained more or less intact
until 1988, when all-day opening during weekdays and at weekends became lawful
(Gourvish, 1997, p 610). These changes also reflected a gathering moral panic over
'free-drinking women'. In this case the 'climate of cultural ambiguity' referred to
the new role experienced by women in society who for the first time were out
at work earning a living, going from factory to pub and acting independently of
men. Essentially, the panic formed around binge drinking, but this itself was an
expression of a wider cultural malaise around the changed roles of women involved
in the war effort. The legislative reaction, however, is a reminder of how panics
serve political and legal ends and have real tangible effects throughout society in
restricting individual freedoms.

So the link between drink and moral panic has a history, but to what extent can
present-day concerns with binge drinking, particularly in reference to youth, be
understood in terms of a moral panic? Moreover, what might this tell us about
fears regarding the wider role of youth in modern society?

Binge drinking: the construction of a 21st-century moral panic?

We are all familiar with newspaper reports and TV images of gangs of drunken
youth staggering from one all-night city pub to the next, fuelled by a 'binge'
of alcohol. As indicated above, the link between youth and drink as a social
problem is not a recent one; the social problems associated with alcoholism have
a long duration and sociologists have a history in researching the wider social
and cultural dynamics of alcoholism from a number of approaches (Bale, 1946;
Bucholz and Robins, 1989; Mitchell, 2007). However, the fear and fascination
with the terminology of 'binge drinking' is a relatively recent phenomenon. The
language of 'binge drinking' first became a topic of nationwide interest in the

US during the 1990s, with particular reference to college students (Wechsler et al, 2000). In Britain 'binge drinking' began to gain media attention later, from around the late 1990s. One of the first reports by the *British Medical Journal* (*BMJ*) was in 1996, but then the topic of binge drinking was marginal to the main topic of the positive health effects of moderate alcohol intake (*British Medical Journal*, 1996). It wasn't until 2002 that the *BMJ* ran articles that placed binge drinking at the centre of analysis and, in terms of a national epidemic, to the fore (*British Medical Journal*, 2002).

Since then, over the past decade, news media coverage conveying negative images of anti-social, binge-drinking youth has gathered pace in the UK. As mentioned above, the tabloid press has led the way with lurid stories about escalating incidents of binge drinking, which soon became thought of as the new 'British disease' involving 'out of control yobs' and 'brash binge drinking ladettes' 'packing casualty wards' at weekends (Nicholls, 2004). The tenor of the popular press is that 'binge Britain ... is quite simply out of control. The police can't cope, the NHS is swamped and it might well be too late to stop the rot' (*The Sun*, 2008). Surveys eagerly devoured, if only partially digested, reveal, for example, how 39% of those aged 18 to 24 admitted getting 'very drunk' on a 'big night out' at least once a month, with men more likely to binge drink than women (48% versus 31%); and how a quarter of adults are binge drinking on a regular basis (Hall, 2005).

The 'quality press' has also been quick to follow suit in the tenor of its reporting. As *The Observer* (Raynor, 2004) reflected, 'Every weekend, Britain's town centres are transformed into scenes of drunken mayhem and soaring levels of violence.' The *Guardian*, meanwhile has urgently drawn attention to the apparent surge in free-spending young women taking part in binge-drinking, enabled by easy access to cheap alcohol and longer licensing hours. And it warns that adolescents in the UK are now 'among Europe's worst in terms of levels of binge drinking' (*Guardian*, 2009). Or, as *The Times* (Smith, 2003) put it, Britain is currently engulfed in 'A culture of heroic alcohol consumption'.

It is interesting to note the pattern of news coverage. Across the news media, reporting of binge drinking increases steadily, reaches a peak, then subsides for no apparent reason, before steadily increasing once again. For example, if we take the online versions of *The Times* and the *Guardian*, we see a pattern of reporting (**Table 6.1**) that suggests not one surge but two, implying that the interest and concern about binge drinking may be cyclical, and more persistent than a one-off process. (As we will explain later, this pattern has implications for understanding binge drinking as a 'moral panic'.)

The UK government, health professionals and binge drinking

Of course, the media have not been alone in proclaiming the image of out-of-control, binge-drinking youth. The government has also expressed a growing concern to combat what it appears to believe is an epidemic of binge drinking in the UK. Drawing together the key findings from previous official reports, a

Table 6.1: Reporting of binge drinking, 2001–09 (no of press reports)

Year	The Times Online	Guardian Online
2001[a]	1	94
2002	16	84
2003	160	170
2004	346	311
2005[b]	420	465
2006	215	182
2007	236	289
2008[c]	291	365

Notes: [a] Initial low rate of reporting, 2001; [b] High rate of reporting for both newspapers, 2005; [c] Beginnings of new surge in reporting, 2008.

government report in 2003 points out the adverse mental health consequences of binge drinking, including increasing levels of suicide and brain malfunction, and the links between binge drinking, anti-social behaviour, street crime, burglary and sexual offences (POST, 2005, pp 1–2). The report goes on to 'suggest' that 23% of adult males and 9% of adult females (a total of 5.9 million people) engage in binge drinking; that 'in the last decade, binge drinking among young British women has increased more than in any other EU country; that UK death rates due to acute intoxication have doubled in the last 20 years in both sexes; and that 29% of deaths attributable to alcohol are from injuries that have occurred in a state of intoxication' (POST, 2005, pp 1–2). The Prime Minister's Strategy Unit's report on alcohol harm noted that per capita consumption in England had increased by 121% since 1951 (Prime Minister's Strategy Unit, 2004, p 13) and summarised that 'as a society we are drinking more, more often. We have particularly high levels of binge drinking amongst 16–24 year olds, and British teenagers are some of the heaviest teenage drinkers in Europe' (Prime Minister's Strategy Unit, 2004, p 27). Scotland, it is argued, 'has a serious problem with drunken and disorderly behaviour', leading to 'unsavoury drinking practices that cost the country £1 billion a year' (Scottish Executive, 2002). Governments in England and Scotland argued for a multi-directional approach to the social problem of binge drinking, involving greater police presence on the streets, stricter licensing laws and the re-education of parents and children about the risks involved in drinking. In 2008 the then Home Secretary, Jacqui Smith, at the launch of a £4 million national advertising campaign against binge drinking, gave notice that the government 'was not prepared to tolerate alcohol-fuelled crime and disorder on our streets and this new campaign will challenge people to think twice about the serious consequences of losing control' (Home Office, 2008a). The Home Office has stated further that the police must have all the powers they need to make groups of young people drinking in public a thing of the past (Home Office, 2008b).

Health professionals, too, have been at the forefront in the battle against a rising tide of binge-drinking youth. The British Medical Association (BMA), for example, is concerned with how 'Recent years have seen increasing interest in the levels of alcohol misuse in the UK, and in particular the pattern of binge drinking and heavy drinking' (BMA, 2008). While the BMA recognises that alcohol is part of our culture and that most individuals consume alcohol 'sensibly', it has, nevertheless, become increasingly concerned with 'the pattern of drinking among adolescents, and the high level of binge drinking and heavy drinking among men and women in the 16 to 24 and 25 to 44 age groups' (BMA Board of Science, 2009). Arguing that alcohol misuse is now an epidemic, the BMA calls on the UK government to 'implement alcohol control policies that are evidence based and proven to reduce alcohol-related harm'. Its call includes policies limiting access to alcohol, the enforcement of responsible retailing and a move away from self-regulation by the alcohol industry (BMA Board of Science, 2009). The Royal College of Nursing (Staines, 2007) has also issued a plea to the government to 'increase taxation on alcohol, ban alcohol advertising before 9pm and in cinemas apart from films rated 18 and reduce the drink driving limit to the EU standard of 0.5g/l and a near zero limit for new drivers', and has urged the government to 'step up public health campaigns' to raise awareness of the dangers of binge drinking (Raper, 2009).

While the social and personal benefits of alcohol consumption are not ignored in this literature, it is fair to say that the central message coming from both media and government reporting by the mid 2000s was that the British public – and especially British youth – is immersed in a 'binge culture' where 'irresponsible drinking habits' are in danger of reaching epidemic proportions. The image is reflected in the language used to describe 'binge drinkers, who are written off and spoken about as 'people who storm bars', are 'defiant drinkers', 'confused about the amount they drink', in a 'state of denial' about their problem and lacking in 'personal responsibility'. We inhabit a 'binge culture' that is 'out of control' and likely to ignite a health 'time bomb', with 'thousands of children being admitted to hospital in England every year because of alcohol-related problems, mental and behavioural disorders' (Paramedic UK, 2004).

But how accurate a picture is being painted here? Without detracting from the very real problems caused by overuse of alcohol, how are we to understand the particular, growing concern with binge-drinking youth? From the above it is clear that the media, health and health-related professionals and the government are all of the belief that a binge-drinking culture is upon us, is out of control and is a potential major threat to the health and well-being of a significant minority, youth in particular. To what extent is the problem of binge drinking being amplified out of all proportion? To what extent are drink issues today any more or less bad than in the past? Are we witnessing a moral panic, as much as a real medical and welfare threat to youth? The rest of this chapter will attempt to address these questions.

'Binge drinking': a problem of definition?

All of the evidence above is based on a variety of definitions of what constitutes binge drinking. While the evidence often produced of drunken sprawls in urban centres at weekends, and the knock-on effects these may have for the health services and the incidence of crime is not in dispute, the question remains: to what extent are we getting an accurate picture of a social issue, and to what extent are definitional issues constitutive of the 'social problem'? We face a dilemma here. The public domain is awash with different definitions of binge drinking as opposed to 'normal' drinking patterns. The following are just a selection of definitions that have been used, and given different emphasis, depending on who is doing the measuring and reporting:

- supping more than five alcoholic drinks in a row at least three times in a month;
- consuming over half the government's recommended number of units for a week in one session (thus, binge drinking would be defined as drinking, in one session, 10 units for men and seven units for women);
- consuming more than five drinks on a single occasion (Alcohol Concern);
- consuming eight or more units for men and six or more units for women on at least one day in the week;
- consuming two-thirds of a bottle of wine for women or four pints of beer for men;
- an extended period of time, usually two days or more, during which a person repeatedly drinks to intoxication, giving up usual activities and obligations;
- consumption of five drinks for males and four drinks for females during one drinking experience in the previous two-week time period.

One would perhaps be forgiven for asking 'what definition is it to be?': is it five drinks in a row three times per month; two consecutive days of 'repeated intoxication; the consumption of four pints and two-thirds of a bottle of wine (and is such a bottle 1 litre or 0.75 litre?); five drinks in a single session; eight or more 'units' one day per week?

The elusive character of binge-drinking definitions does not stop here, but extends to differences between one nation and another. For example, in their research into social inequalities in patterns of alcohol consumption across different countries, Bloomfield et al (2006) reflected on just how variable definitions are; for example, 'three or more glasses in Hungary, five or more glasses on one occasion in Germany, Israel, Sweden, Brazil, Mexico, six or more glasses on one occasion in Finland and The Netherlands, or eight or more glasses in Switzerland'. Similarly, in their overview of conceptual ambiguities regarding binge drinking, Herring et al (2008, pp 477–8) concluded that,

> although the term 'binge drinking' is common place in contemporary
> society, there is no consensus definition of binge drinking and it has

been used to describe quite different patterns of drinking. The use of the term has also changed over time from a lengthy period of intoxication over days in the 1940s and 50s to a defined episode now. There is plainly a great deal of confusion surrounding the term binge drinking and this raises questions about its usefulness.

Indeed, given the lack of a clear and creditable definition, it is perhaps little wonder that more than 50% of individuals accused of 'binging' either deny that they are doing any such thing or are completely unaware that they are doing so (BUPA, 2005).

Moreover, the way in which society approaches heavy drinking varies according to the social context that actually defines drinking as 'heavy' or 'binge', or whether the drinking is something undertaken in prolonged bouts or single sessions; a point also raised by Herring's research (Herring et al, 2008). So it is interesting to note that how we think about and react to drinking depends on the historical and social context. For example, in the 1960s and 1970s there was an equally strong drinking culture among working-class communities in the UK. The context was one of full employment, steady working hours and rising disposable income, which influenced the culture of weekend nights out on the town in which heavy drinking played a central role. In this cultural context, while problems of heavy drinking existed and caused real personal and family distress for some, in general this heavy drinking culture was not frowned upon in the way it is today, and was certainly not called the pejorative name of 'binge drinking'. It was more an accepted way of living, or at least this was the stereotypical image painted of certain working-class communities in the media. Sometimes not living up to the image was more of an issue for individuals.

If one adds this example of cultural ambiguity regarding perceptions of drinking to the lack of a clear and discernible definition of the difference between drinking and 'binge drinking', then one may wonder where the line between reality and rhetoric is being drawn. The popular press, as one might perhaps expect, has presented binge drinking in sensational terms, but what is less obvious is why health-related professional bodies, government and sections of the wider public have joined it in fixating on the issue of binge drinking. Below, we assess the argument that the current focus on binge drinking can be understood as a moral panic, and from here we draw out the wider implications of such an understanding for issues of social control.

Binge drinking: a classic case of moral panic?

The media, government and health professionals assume that binge drinking is an objective social problem to be cured or managed and controlled. To recall a question that we raised at the beginning of this chapter: to what extent is this a classic example of the medicalisation of a social problem that has its origins in wider social structures – invoking the distinction raised by C.R. Wright Mills (1959) between *personal troubles* and *public issues*? As noted, Mills argued that individuals experience problems and challenges that they can influence and change, and which they and others feel responsible for resolving. Mills defined these as *personal troubles*, but noted that more often than not the problems and challenges facing individuals are manifestations of *public issues* originating in larger social institutions and structures that individuals have little power to control and fundamentally change. The definitional and cultural ambiguities outlined above will perhaps alert us to another way of looking at binge drinking, one that is more concerned with how certain behaviours become 'social problems', and for whom. Arguably, to answer the question requires us to uncover the social and bureaucratic forces that recognise and define, and so 'bring in to being', social problems such as binge drinking, forces that are 'involved in a symbolic campaign that may reflect the interests of particular movements and pressure groups, regardless of the objective basis of the alleged dangers' (Jenkins, 1992, p 3).

In terms of the deviancy amplification model outlined earlier in this chapter (see **Figure 6.1**), we can perhaps view a similar pattern in the interest in binge-drinking youth and its status as a moral panic. For example, there has been no shortage of specific claim makers wishing to link youth drinking with binge drinking; as we observed earlier, medical journals and the popular press overlap in their labelling of youth drinking patterns as an 'epidemic of binge drinking' and in broadcasting this message to the wider society in a manner guaranteed to invoke a negative reaction – especially given the close association invoked between binge-drinking culture and crime. We also observed how the 'deviant group' in question – 'youth binge drinkers' – often resisted the claim makers' definitions of their drinking habits as 'binge drinking'. One also notes how the label 'binge drinker' and the massive media attention given to binge-drinking cultures has the possible knock-on effect of encouraging those youth who do drink to live up to the label; all, perhaps, evidence of the beginning of a 'deviancy spiral'. Deviancy then spirals to a new level via the assumed links that health authority professionals highlight between binge drinking and threats to health, leading to a situation in which calls for tighter drinking laws and tighter control over youth and their 'anti-social' behaviours gain ground, to the point where governments step in with legislation.

Binge drinking, moral panics and the wider climate of 'cultural ambiguities'

Earlier in this chapter we took a historical detour to look at past moral panics about excessive drinking. This detour reminds us of a key argument put forward by Cohen, that moral panics express wider social changes – which for us begs the question of how one should understand the *current* binge-drinking panic. Cohen writes of a 'climate of cultural ambiguity' to describe periods of social change and uncertainty. What 'climate of cultural ambiguity' is present today to which moral panics surrounding binge drinking give rise?

We know that the panic and fears associated with binge drinking are very much centred on *youth*. Youth today stands at the crossroads of a number of overlapping social problems, including 'anti-social behaviour', binge drinking and crime. So what is it about youth today that gives rise to uncertainty and risk and so much general anxiety? Following Cohen, one might say that youth are acquiring the status of modern-day 'folk-devils'. But the question is why? It was explained earlier that Hall's approach to the concept of moral panic identifies the wider ideological significance of moral panics. How are we to understand this in relation to binge drinking?

One issue worth considering, in this respect, is the adverse changes to the perceived stability of the transition from childhood to youth and through to adulthood? Until the early 1980s, social norms regarding the developmental milestones of the life cycle were fairly well regulated through the relationship between the family, education and employment. In the decades since, however, the once stable relationship between these institutions has been seriously threatened and has become a source of uncertainty. The transition from home to education and qualification, and on to employment and career possibilities, which once marked out the transition from youth to adulthood is no longer guaranteed, and has become a source of uncertainty in which the fear of failure is strong and insecurities about the role of youth grow.

In particular, any notion of a traditional nuclear family has now been overtaken by diverse patterns of family life. Education no longer leads in a relatively straightforward manner to employment, but for a significant minority of youth it may instead lead simply to a revolving door of more education, low-quality skills and training courses, poorly paid or careerless employment, and full circle back to a culture of lifelong learning. Moreover, by the mid 1980s chronic long-term unemployment and a significant rise in work intensity and part-time, casual and often poorly paid work had become a fact of life, for youth in particular (Tomaney, 1990). Since then, youth have become the target of stricter benefit regimes (Finn, 1997) and an endless cycle of workfare initiatives (benefits paid to take up training courses), including the Youth Opportunities Scheme and the Youth Training Scheme in the 1980s and 1990s (Bonefeld, 1992), followed by the New Labour government's New Deal and Welfare to Work programmes for youth aged 19–24 years. In sum, the concept of youth and its relation to a future characterised by social mobility, career development and independence has been broken and replaced by the link to insecurity, social problems and anti-social threats.

Both Conservative and Labour governments placed (and continue to place) the lion's share of responsibility for being 'jobless' on the individuals themselves, by either directly or tacitly reasoning that they were (are) a 'work-shy' 'underclass', bereft of the 'work ethic', 'dependants', 'scroungers', a significant minority of whom were going to some lengths to defraud the state by making bogus benefit claims, or deliberately getting pregnant so as to gain access to more welfare services, and so on (Mead, 1997). The reality of poor training and lack of job opportunities beyond the poorly paid work available in the youth labour market has led to the development of a situation whereby a significant minority of youth are opting out of the formal institutions of education, training and work, the so-called NEETs: not in employment, education or training.

The above context may perhaps be read as a crisis for society, expressed in the form of a series of moral panics about youth as 'a present problem' to be 'contained', rather than a hope for the future. 'Youth' has more often been associated with the future, with hope and social progress. Today it would seem to attract more negative connotations as a source of danger, criminality, deviance and threat to the work ethic. If youth signifies aspirations of social progress and the future, yet society cannot apparently guarantee a stable career path, then youth stand in a very precarious position, one that is perhaps more liable for negative labelling and moral panic. As we have seen, society is less willing to deal with these wider social issues and perhaps more inclined to seek solutions by transforming them, through moral panics, into personal failings and medical issues. As a result, the central message of both media and government reporting by the mid 2000s was that the British public and especially British youth were ensconced in a 'binge culture' in which 'irresponsible drinking habits' were in danger of reaching epidemic proportions, an image which is reflected in the emotive language used to describe 'binge drinkers'.

Conclusion

This chapter has examined the concept of moral panic as another way of representing the dynamics involved in the medicalisation of society. The example of binge-drinking youth was developed to explain how moral panics promote the medicalisation of society by converting social structural maladies into seemingly more manageable and resolvable personal failings and medically related matters underpinning binge drinking. Drawing on evidence from the media, health professionals and government sources, the chapter has explained how each of these sources treats binge drinking as something objective to be either cured or controlled. While the real negative consequences of alcohol excess are never in doubt, the chapter also argued that social problems are never neutrally observed, nor do they exist as objects of investigation. Social issues and problems are also the source of social construction, and these constructions tend to express social anxieties, fears and insecurities, which may also echo broader structural changes.

The concept of moral panic has been criticised for, among other things, seeming to deny the objective reality of a social issue. However, to argue the case for moral panic does not mean that a social issue does not exist; more accurately, it means that how that issue is framed as a problem is the result of social construction. The chapter also considered the connection between society's conception of youth as a social problem and society's difficulties in guaranteeing employment and social advancement. By embedding binge drinking in wider social structural changes the chapter has attempted to articulate the nature of binge drinking as both an objective reality and an object of social construction.

While the chapter has focused attention on binge drinking in order to explore the concept of moral panic, it is worth stressing that panics about binge-drinking may also be explained as part of an increasing number of moral panics that sweep across society until a situation arises where one can say that panic is endemic and of a generalised nature. In this respect, Thompson (1998) has argued that moral panics have become increasingly common in society, to the degree that we are effectively 'living in the age of the moral panic'. For some, this 'age' is bound up with a wider *politics of fear* that embraces youth but also covers the wider population. Furedi (2005), for example, has argued that one reason why we fear so much is because life is dominated by competing groups of *fear entrepreneurs* who promote their cause, stake their claims or sell their products by using fear. Politicians, the media, businesses, environmental organisations, public health officials and advocacy groups are continually warning us about something new to fear.

> ... fear entrepreneurs serve to transform our anxieties about life into tangible fears. Every major event becomes the focus for competing claims about what you need to fear. (Furedi, 2005)

When fear loses touch with something specific to fear, such as starvation or being homeless, then it breeds an unfocused sense of anxiety that can attach itself to anything. Take, for example, fear of crime. We live in a society in which crime appears to be all around us, posing a constant source of threat to our safety. Yet how often are we personally affected by crime? Crime is, moreover, class specific, most of it being experienced by those lower down the class hierarchy of modern society. Yet it appears as and is spoken about in terms of an *omnipotent risk* to which all are potentially exposed.

Furedi suggests that we live in a *culture of fear* that provides fertile ground for endless cycles of moral panics. This culture of fear is produced in part by industries who sell 'security' through the marketing of fear: health insurance, legal insurance, IT companies selling anti-virus products; each prospers from the collective sense of anxiety they help create. Every adverse event is amplified into a potential catastrophe, human tragedy or unmanageable risk, inducing and sustaining a culture of free-floating fear without an object, settling here and settling there, invoking the latest moral panic. The ease with which we reach for an 'apocalyptic vocabulary' to render meaning to everyday social issues speaks volumes about our perception of ourselves in late modernity. We are quick to label behaviours as 'anti-social' or events as out-of-control 'epidemics' or 'syndromes'.

Furedi has argued that 'the fear market thrives in an environment where society has internalised the belief that since people are too powerless to cope with the risks they face, we are continually confronted with the problem of survival. This mood of powerlessness has encouraged a market where different fears compete with one another in order to capture the public imagination' (Furedi, 2005).

For Furedi, the modern era is one in which a politics of fear promotes a culture of victimhood and individual powerlessness when one is confronted by a constant diet of moral panic, which in turn creates a culture of fear capable of moving from one focus (health scare) this month to another focus (binge drinking) another month. Moreover, what is so politically powerful is the manner in which fear floats from one issue to another, combining and connecting them. So, for example, the manner in which binge drinking is linked to health hazards, anti-social behaviour and crime. The media act as the amplifier but not the creator of panics and fears. In this respect, fear can be employed to coerce deviant groups and to maintain public order. Through provoking a common reaction to a perceived threat it can also provide focus for gaining consensus and unity. The politics of fear works by depoliticising social issues such as, in our case, binge-drinking youth, reducing these issues *to* the status of psychological traumas or individual fears, and demonising the group concerned.

Questions for further reflection

1   Outline the problems involved in defining 'binge drinking'.
2   Thinking back to Chapter Five, compare and contrast the concepts of 'risk society' and 'moral panic' as a way of explaining the fear and fascination with binge drinking.
3   Provide five reasons why public trust in medical science may be lessening.

References

Bale, R.F. (1946) 'Cultural differences in rates of alcoholism', *Quarterly Journal of Studies on Alcohol*, vol 6, pp 480–99.

Bloomfield, K. et al (2006) 'Social inequalities in alcohol consumption and alcohol-related problems in the study countries of the EU concerted action "Gender, culture and alcohol problems: a multi-national study"', *Alcohol & Alcoholism*, vol 41, Supplement 1, pp i26–i36.

BMA (British Medical Association) (2008) *Alcohol misuse – tackling the UK epidemic, Briefing paper on the 2008 report*, March (www.bma.org.uk/health_promotion_ethics/alcohol/Alcoholmisuserpt.jsp#3).

BMA Board of Science (2009) *Memorandum of evidence from the BMA to the Health Select Committee inquiry on alcohol*, www.bma.org.uk/health_promotion_ethics/alcohol/alcoholevid.jsp.

British Medical Journal (1996) Editorial: 'Sensible drinking', *British Medical Journal*, vol 312, p 1.

British Medical Journal (2002) News roundup, 'Scotland produces plan to tackle binge drinking', vol 324, p 190.

Bonefeld, W. (1992) *The recomposition of the British state in the 1980s*, Aldershot: Dartmouth Publishing.

Bucholz, K.K. and Robins, L.N. (1989) 'Sociological research on alcohol use, problems, and policy', *Annual Review of Sociology*, vol 15, p 1636.

BUPA (British United Patients' Association) (2005) 'A quarter of all UK adults are binge drinkers', 27 October (www.bupa.co.uk/about/html/pr/271005_binge_drinking.html).

Cohen, S. (2002) *Folk devils and moral panics* (3rd edn), London: Routledge.

Finn, D. (1997) 'Labour's new deal for the unemployed: making it work locally', *Local Economy,* vol 12, no 3, November, pp 247–58.

Furedi, F. (2005) 'The market in fear', *Spiked Online*, September (www.spiked-online.com/Articles/0000000CAD7B.htm).

Goode, E. and Ben-Yehuda, N. (2009) *Moral panics: The social construction of deviance*, Oxford: Blackwell Publishing.

Gourvish, T.R. (1997) 'The business of alcohol in the US and the UK: UK regulation and drinking habits, 1914–39', *Business and Economic History*, vol 26, no 2, pp 609–16.

Guardian (2009) Editorial: 'Binge drinking: teenage kicks', 27 March.

Hall, S. (1978) *Policing the crisis: Mugging, the state and law and order*, Basingstoke: Palgrave Macmillan.

Hall, W. (2005) 'Quarter of adults "are binge drinkers"', *Daily Telegraph* (http://news.telegraph.co.uk/news/main.jhtml?xml=/news/2005/10/27/nbinge27.xml).

Halle, S. (2002) 'New wave of "sophisticated" alcopops fuels teenage binge drinking', *Guardian*, 14 December.

Herring, R. et al (2008) 'Binge drinking: an exploration of a confused concept', *Journal of Epidemiology and Community Health*, vol 62, pp 476–91.

Hier, S.P. (2003) 'Risk and panic in late modernity: implications of the converging sites of social anxiety', *British Journal of Sociology*, vol 54, no 1, pp 3–20.

Home Office (2008a) 'Launch of new multi-million binge drinking advertising campaign', 17 June (http://press.homeoffice.gov.uk/press-releases/Binge-Drinking-Campaign).

Home Office (2008b) 'Tougher powers to tackle teen drinkers', 6 February (http://press.homeoffice.gov.uk/press-releases/drinking).

Hunt, T. (2004) 'After 13 centuries of binge-drinking we've found a new excuse', *Sunday Times*, 24 March.

Jenkins, P. (1992) *Intimate enemies: Moral panics in contemporary Great Britain: social problems and social issues*, New York, NY: Walter Paperback, Aldine Transaction.

Mead, L.M. (1997) *From welfare to work, lessons from America*, London: IEA.

Mills, C.W. (1959) *The sociological imagination*, New York: Oxford University Press.

Mitchell, T. (2007) *Intoxicated identities*, London: Taylor & Francis.

Nicholls, J. (2004) 'Drink, the new British disease?', *History Today*, vol 60, no 1, pp 10–17.

Observer (2004) 'On the streets of binge Britain', 5 September.

Paramedic UK (2004) 'Teenage binge drinking out-of-control', April (www.paramedic.org.uk/news_archive/2004/04/News_Item.2004–04–28.4719/view).

POST (2005) 'Binge drinking and public health', postnote, July, no 244 (www. parliament.uk/documents/upload/postpn244.pdf).

Prime Minister's Strategy Unit (2004) *Alcohol harm reduction strategy for England*, (www.cabinetoffice.gov.uk/media/cabinetoffice/strategy/assets/caboffce%20 alcoholhar.pdf).

Raper, V. (2009) 'Nurses call on government to tackle binge drinking', Nursingtimes.net, 22 July (www.nursingtimes.net/nursing-practice-clinical-research/clinical-subjects/alcohol/nurses-call-on-government-to-tackle-binge-drinking/5004322.article).

Raynor, J. (2004) 'On the streets of Binge Britain', *The Observer*, 5 September.

Roberts, B.B. and Groenendijik, L.F. (2005) 'Moral panic and Holland's libertine youth of the 1650s and 1660s', *Journal of Family History*, vol 30, no 4, p 327.

Scottish Executive (2002) 'Scottish national alcohol strategy calls time on binge drinking' (www.ias.org.uk/resources/publications/alcoholalert/alert200201/ al200201_p 9.html).

Smith, J. (2003) 'A culture of heroic alcohol consumption', *The Timesonline*, (www. timesonline.co.uk/tol/life_and_style/article1098355.ece).

Staines, R. (2007) 'RCN signs up to anti-drink campaign', *Nursingtimes.net*, 14 November (www.nursingtimes.net/whats-new-in-nursing/rcn-signs-up-to-anti-drink-campaign/263241.article).

Sun (2008) Lorraine Kelly, 'Booze Britain, it's a plague' (www.thesun.co.uk/sol/ homepage/news/columnists/lorraine_kelly/864639/Experts-helped-kill-tot-Jessica.html).

Thompson. K. (1998) *Moral panics*, London: Routledge.

Tomaney, J. (1990) 'The reality of workplace flexibility', *Capital and Class*, no 40, pp 29–60.

Wechsler, H. et al (2000) 'College binge drinking in the 1990s: a continuing problem. Results of the Harvard School of Public Health 1999 College Alcohol Study', *Journal of American College Health*, vol 48, no 5, pp 199–210.

SEVEN

Contesting paradigms in the medicalisation of obesity

The transformation from fat to thin, immoral to upright, deviant to obedient, divides the body within itself. (Spitzack, 1987, p 363)

If I were permitted to abolish six of the deadly sins from our planet the one which I would retain is gluttony. People who are driven by pride, wrath, envy, lust, or avarice probably make life unpleasant for those around them, but the penalties associated with gluttony and sloth (which are often mentioned together) fall mainly on the sinners themselves. (Garrow, 1996)

... focusing on fast food alone is a narrow approach to curbing the much-publicised obesity epidemic. (Brindal et al, 2008, p 115)

Introduction

Towards the end of the last chapter we noted how, in the present era, every adverse event is amplified into a potential catastrophe, human tragedy or unmanageable risk, to induce and sustain a culture of free-floating fear without an object, settling here and settling there, invoking the latest moral panic. The ease with which we reach for an 'apocalyptic vocabulary' to render meaning to everyday social issues speaks volumes about our perception of ourselves in late modernity. We are quick to label behaviours as 'anti-social' or events as out-of-control 'epidemics' or 'syndromes'. So it is with obesity. We are often confronted by media and government reports that obesity is fast attaining the status of an epidemic. Debate continues over the complex causalities involved in this 'epidemic'. It is widely accepted that the aetiology of obesity is a complex determination of genetic, lifestyle and wider social factors. However, different degrees of importance have been ascribed to either one or another factor. For example, the dominant medical paradigm, while aware of social structural factors such as the powerful influence of a fast-food industry and culture, tends to reflect the biomedical view that obesity is an illness and, as with most illnesses, causes, and so cures, are focused on the body and individual behaviour (Prentice and Jebb, 1995). For those who lay emphasis on social structural factors, such as, for example, the effects on the individual of consumer society, broader shifts from industrial to post-industrial society and the 'McDonaldisation' of the food chain, biology and lifestyle play only marginal roles. The social structuralist paradigm would argue that the medical response medicalises what is, overwhelmingly, a social structurally generated phenomenon. In this sense, the narrative is similar to the discussion of binge drinking in the last chapter. However, in this chapter we note an underlying unity between medical and social structural paradigms of the causes generating an obesity epidemic. This underlying unity is down to both paradigms treating obesity as a fact, whether biological or social. This chapter highlights the way in which these two conceptual approaches legitimise talk of obesity epidemics as 'factual'. In opposition to this, the chapter then draws on the social constructionist paradigm to evaluate the extent to which both of these responses are implicated in the dual process of medicalising obesity and fashioning forms of social control over the body.

To do so, the chapter is structured as follows. It:

- outlines the official definition of obesity and describes recent statistical trends that emerge from this definition;
- identifies three paradigms for understanding obesity: medical, social structural and social construction;
- argues that the medical paradigm, covering the matrix of biological causation, medical and dietary interventions, offers key insights into obesity, but that in not incorporating social structural factors it fails to provide a convincing explanation;
- evaluates the argument of the social paradigm that wider social structures are the primary causes of obesity and explains how both the medical and social paradigms share the underlying assumption that obesity is real, something that can be measured and 'cured';
- explains the social constructionist paradigm and its claim that obesity is constructed by both the medical and social paradigms as a means of medicalising social issues and advancing social control of the body;
- concludes by arguing that all three paradigms are crucial to an understanding of why obesity is a key issue in contemporary society.

Measuring obesity

The official classification of what is 'normal', 'over' and 'obese' weight is the body mass index or BMI. The BMI calculates weight and height for adults and weight, height and age for children. The BMI for an adult (over 20 years) falls into one of the categories listed in **Table 7.1**. Adults are considered to be obese if they are more than 20% over their normal weight range (Garrow and Webster, 1985). The measurement of child obesity is age-dependent relative to growth and development.

According to statistical trends based on the BMI measurement, the upward trends in overweight and obesity levels look alarming. The World Health Organization (WHO, 2005) estimates that, globally, 1.6 billion adults are now overweight and up to 400 million adults are obese, and has projected that by 2015 these figures

Table 7.1: Weight categories as calculated by the Body Mass Index

BMI	Weight status
Below 18.5	Underweight
18.5–24.9	Normal
25.0–29.9	Overweight
30.0 and above	Obese

Note: BMI = $\dfrac{\text{(weight in pounds)} \times 703}{\text{(height in inches)} \times \text{(height in inches)}}$

will rise to 2.3 billion and 700 million respectively. Of course, global estimates differ regionally for both child and adult obesity, but the trend is upward.

Take child obesity. In the US one estimate suggests that between 1963 and 2000 the rates of child obesity rose from 4% to 16% for the age group 6–11 years and from 5% to 16% for the age group 12–19 years, with later estimates indicating that 'approximately nine million children over 6 years of age are considered obese (Institute of Medicine, 2004, p 1). In the European Union it is estimated that 'the number of children who are overweight or obese … is now rising at more than 400,000 a year and when accession countries are included the rate of children overweight or obese is one in four; which is a higher rate than had been expected based on original trends in the 80s and is already higher than the predicted peak for 2010' (Commission of the European Communities, 2005). In the UK, NHS data estimate that 10.4% of boys and 8.8% of girls beginning primary school (aged 4–5 years) and 20% of boys and 16.6% of girls (average 18.3%) towards the end of primary school (aged 10–11 years) are obese (NHS, 2009).

With respect to growing rates of adult obesity, a US government survey of adults in 2002–03 estimated that up to 66% of adults were either overweight or obese (NHANES, 2006). If we leave out 'overweight and take obesity levels alone, then the long term trend has been markedly upward as rates of obesity in the US are estimated to have almost trebled from 13% in the 1960s to 35% by the mid-2000s' (NCHS, 2008, p 2). Breaking these figures down from state to state, then only one US state (Colorado) had a prevalence of obesity less than 20%. 'Thirty US states had a prevalence of obesity which was equal to or greater than 25%; three of these states (Alabama, Mississippi and Tennessee) had a prevalence rate equal to or greater than 30%.' (International Obesity Taskforce, 2009). A similar picture emerges across the European Union, where 'adult obesity ranges from 10% to 27% in men and up to 38% in women' (Commission of the European Communities, 2005).

In Britain, estimates record a long-term upward trend in levels of adult obesity. The number of obese adults was estimated to be 7% in 1980 and doubled by the mid 1990s to 13% of men and 16% of women (MacIntyre, 1998, p 77). By 2002 the Chief Medical Officer for England (CMO, 2002) reported that 'Obesity levels in England have tripled in the past two decades; around a fifth (21 per cent) of men and a quarter (24 per cent) of women are now obese, while almost 24 million adults are now overweight or obese.' The report noted that 'obesity is also rising among children – in the five years between 1996 and 2001, the proportion of obese children aged 6 to 15 years rose by some 3.5 per cent'.

More recent estimates suggest that adult obesity levels have increased in England and Wales to approximately 24% for both men and women, a figure that is estimated to rise in future decades, as reflected in the continued upward trend in the medium BMI measurement (Foresight, 2007, p 25); while in Scotland the percentage for men has increased to 22% and 24% for women (Scottish Health Survey, 2003). Indeed, the UK government became so concerned about the rising trends in obesity that Alan Johnson, then UK Secretary of State for Health, felt compelled to warn how

> [today], two thirds of all adults and one third of all children are either overweight or obese. By 2050, on current trends these figures will rise to almost nine in ten adults and two thirds of all children. By then, obesity, which is already responsible for 9000 premature deaths each year, 58 per cent of all type 2 diabetes, 21 per cent of heart disease and a 9 year reduction in life expectancy, will lead to a seven-fold increase in direct health costs with wider costs to society of around £50 billion. (Johnson, 2008)

Taken together, the above trends paint an alarming picture of rising levels of obesity. What, then, are the causes of this trend and what role do biological and social factors play? Moreover, is the BMI scale an adequate indicator around which to compile statistical trends, and do the data reflect real trends or are they being manipulated or socially constructed? If so, how does this relate to power and body politics? What we do know is that it is widely accepted among those who share the view of a growing obesity epidemic that the aetiology of obesity is a complex determination of genetic, lifestyle and wider social factors. However, as mentioned earlier, different degrees of importance have been ascribed to either one or another of these factors. For example, the dominant medical response, while aware of social structural factors like the powerful influence of the fast-food industry and culture, tends to reflect the biomedical view that obesity is an illness and, as with most illnesses, causes and so cures are focused on the body and individual behaviour (Prentice and Jebb, 1995). Hence cures, such as the search for the obese gene, anti-obesity drugs and dietary advice are directed towards the body and the individual. For conceptual clarity we can term this the *medical paradigm*. Likewise, those who lay emphasis on social structural factors such as, for example, the effects on the individual of consumer society, broader shifts from industrial to post-industrial society and the 'McDonaldisation' of the food chain, also recognise that biology and lifestyles can play their part. Yet their solutions tend to place priority on society-wide policies that affect broader social changes in the way we eat and live. Again for conceptual clarity, this can be termed the *social structural paradigm.* Below we first consider the causes and solutions offered by the medical paradigm.

The medical paradigm

As mentioned above, the medical paradigm encompasses a genetic approach to obesity that embraces medical interventions and dietary technologies. At the same time it is aware of, but tends to play down, the social factors. Research has been shown to ignore the ability of people to be reflexive about how they present themselves to other people, researchers included. For example, in the 1970s research into poor metabolism, which was seen as a key factor in the prevention of a balance between food intake and energy expenditure, became less convincing as a result of the recognition that individuals tend to conceal or underestimate the actual amount of calories they consume. The capacity for reflexivity, in effect, inserted an unknown element into the equation between intake and energy expenditure (Lichtman et al, 1992; Prentice and Jebb, 1995). Moreover, the relationship between food intake, energy expenditure and resulting homeostasis in terms of body weight has since been shown to be more fluid than was first thought. Science is able to reveal a relative metabolic *settling point* between appetite and body weight regulation, influenced by the broader environment, rather than a *fixed set point* (Ruppel Shell, 2003, p 221).

More recently, epidemiological studies have investigated the causal influence of hormones and their mass production in pharmaceutically manufactured cures. For example, the discovery of fat hormone leptin in 1993 purported to reveal how low or high levels of leptin, or even the inability to produce it, were associated with weight: low levels with obesity, high levels with thinness. It was argued that leptin regulates the levels of protein related to the registering of appetite to the brain, with low levels increasing appetite and high levels decreasing appetite. It was found, for example, that in some cases of extreme obesity individuals did not have the capacity to generate leptin. However, to complicate things it was also found that plenty of obese people had high levels of leptin. This confirmed that, although leptin is a crucial hormone linked to appetite/weight changes, other factors are involved in the mediation between the hormone and the relationship between appetite and the brain. For example, how hormones behave depends also on a complex array of molecular receptors which could be over- or under-sensitive, depending on the environment within which they operate, which includes biological, psychological and social environmental factors. Adverse psychological circumstance could, for example, induce an environment which inhibited key leptin receptors from doing their job, and hence override messages of satiation. Therefore, while the discovery of leptin is significant, the pathway between it and obesity is a very complex one that also takes in a range of bio-psychosocial factors (Ruppel Shell, 2003). Indeed, the link between obesity and biology becomes even more tenuous if we consider that 'escalating rates of obesity are occurring in a relatively constant gene pool' (Prentice and Jebb,1995). It appears to be the case that the relative settling point in body weight regulation is increasing, due largely to wider environmental factors.

Yet within the medical paradigm the response has been to concentrate more on medical interventions and dietary technology; for example, developing over-the-counter anti-obesity drugs that act on the central nervous system to control appetite, such as Meridiam, Pondimin and Redux; and also Xenical, which acts on the gut to restrict the ability to metabolise fat, thus leading to weight reduction by the generation of nausea, dissuading over-indulgence in fatty food. As Ruppel Shell (2003, p 143) explains: 'Since Xenical blocks about one-third of the fat in the food you eat, you may experience fat with oily discharge, increased bowel movements, and urgent need to have them and an inability to control them, particularly after meals containing more fat than recommended ... Xenical packs a one-two punch – it prevents the body from absorbing part of consumed fat and it discourages those who use it from eating more than the recommended amount of fat in the first place.'

The diet industry has also diversified, providing devices involved in anti-obesity surgery. Medical companies have developed implants that zap the stomach and surrounding nerves with an electrical current, in 'the belief that the electric jolts can help modify eating behaviour, possibly by regulating appetite signals or boosting metabolism' (Spencer, 2005).

The medical paradigm also overlaps with a growing diet industry. Here social agents are seen as constrained by their biology, but also able to make choices to change unhealthy dietary and lifestyle behaviours. It is estimated that in the US 25% of men and 45% of women are on a diet on any given day; 80% of women are dissatisfied with their appearance; 51% of 9- and 10-year-old girls feel better about themselves if they are on a diet and 35% of 'normal dieters' progress to pathological dieting (NEDAI, 2002, p 137). In the US, the weight-loss industry is huge, comprising dozens of eating regimens, dieting support groups, supplements, food products, meal replacements, books and videos. It was estimated that the diet industry would grow from £51 billion in 1996 to £61 billion by 2006 in the US alone (Carvel, 2002). A similar picture emerges in Europe, where, 'If current trends endure, the diet industry will grow from a value of 93 billion euros to 101.1 billion by 2007 within the EU' (DMCPRS, 2003).

In summary, the medical paradigm continues to offer important insights into the causes of and cures for obesity. However, it is fraught with limitations. For example, the reliance on seeking out an obese gene, as we noted earlier in the case of leptin, comes up against the reality that how our genes behave depends also on a complex array of molecular receptors which could be over- or under-sensitive, depending on the environment within which they operate. This includes biological, psychological and social environmental factors. Adverse psychological circumstance could, for example, induce an environment which inhibited key leptin receptors from doing their job, and hence override messages of satiation. Therefore, while the discovery of leptin is significant, the pathway between it and obesity is a very complex one and must take in the range of bio-psychosocial factors (Ruppel Shell, 2003). Indeed, the link between obesity and individual genetics becomes even more tenuous if we consider that 'escalating rates of obesity are occurring in a relatively constant gene pool' (Prentice and Jebb, 1995).

One might draw the conclusion that the desire on the part of paying customers to achieve quick-fix solutions and avoid the stigma of obesity, on the one hand, and the equally strong impulse to make profits, on the other hand, are such strong motive forces within the medical paradigm that they override wider concerns about the long-term viability of diet fads and the attendant risks to health, and marginalise the mounting evidence of wider social causes of obesity. We now explore this within the framework of the social structural paradigm.

The social structural paradigm

As discussed earlier, the social structural paradigm does not rule out medical and dietary solutions, but tends to place priority on wider social changes as more important for understanding the causes of and potential solutions to obesity. Earlier it was suggested that the relative settling point in body weight regulation is increasing, due largely to wider environmental factors. We can now return to this point in relation to wider social processes. According to the social structural paradigm, one reason, among others, that the impact of diets is at best short term is because sustained weight loss and weight-loss maintenance are also very much related to quality-of-life issues surrounding socioeconomic circumstances (Sarlio-Lähteenkorva, 2001). The principal argument coming from the social structural paradigm is that we need to confront the wider social causes of obesity. Principal among these is the idea that industrial society, based on manual labour and less labour-saving technology, is giving way to a post-industrial society where advances in IT mean that information and knowledge flows allow us to fax, phone or e-mail rather than walk and talk; where the car and the shopping mall have taken the place of local shopping; and where technological developments at work have changed energy expenditure, relatively less human labour power being expended in making more goods and services. It is suggested that the post-industrial landscape in which we now live is one where we tend to expend fewer calories in working and tend to walk far less. At the same time we also require more private and public forms of transport because of the tendency for the distance between where we live and where we work to be much greater (Crossley, 2004).

Moreover, what remain central to the post-industrial landscape are cultural changes to the way we consume food, related to the deleterious influence on our diet of the fast-food industry. Multinational fast-food brands such as Burger King, McDonald's, Little Caesars, Subway, and Benny and Jerry's are now a larger part of the high street landscape. It is estimated that the industry 'increased from about 30 000 in 1970 to more than 233 000 locations in the US in 2004', corresponding to an increase in the amount of money spent on food outside the home from 25% of total money spent on food in 1970 to 47.5% of the total spent in 1999, which was projected to increase to about 53% by 2010 (Rosenheck, 2008, p 1). Burger King has about 11,000 outlets in Europe, while McDonald's has in excess of 30,000 outlets worldwide and a customer base of 43 million (Walsh, 2001). According to one source, 'gross profit margins on fast food, defined as sales less the costs of food and labour, range from 30% to 35%, which compares to an average of 15% in non-food merchandise' (Halverson, 1993).

It is argued that the rise of the fast-food industry is strongly associated with the rise in obesity levels over the same period. A recent study of 3,000 young people over 15 years of age found that individuals who frequently ate fast food gained '10 pounds more than those who did so less often, and were more than twice as likely to develop an insulin disorder linked to diabetes' (*Food & Drink Weekly*, 2005).

The fast-food industry, it is argued, fills

> shops, pubs, restaurants and high-street takeaways with high-fat, sugar-rich junk food, and fills the media with propaganda to persuade us and our children to eat it....The manufacturers of fizzy drinks, crisps and sweets (of which sales have risen at least 25-fold since the 1950s) have a vested interest in promoting the idea that we can eat what we like as long as we go to the gym. (*New Statesman*, 2004)

Schlosser (2002) points out how the fast-food industry is dominated by multinational food companies who exert a powerful negative influence on people's livelihoods, on food science and on the food chain. In particular, the fast-food industry operates

> french fry plants in a number of different regions, constantly shifting production to take advantage of the lowest potato prices. The economic fortunes of individual farmers or local communities matter little in the grand scheme. The same practices are true in the ranching, poultry, and hog industries.... Flavorists in laboratories concoct the 'natural and artificial flavors' found in almost every processed food product. McDonald's infuses its fries and chicken sandwiches with essences that mimic beef tallow. A milkshake's strawberry flavour is more likely to come from a test tube than from actual fruit. (Schlosser, 2002, p 119)

Others point to the influence of the fast-food industry on eating habits, as we now eat in less and eat out much more. There has, for example, been a decrease in breakfasts at home, with the growth in 'deskfasts' for those who increasingly choose to eat on the way to work or while at work. The growth in flexi-work time and the faster pace of life have provided the context for drawing people away from the traditional breakfast (*Eurofood*, 2002a).

The fast-food industry has extended its reach into most areas of our lives, to the point where, if we don't come to it, it will find us! It is estimated that schoolchildren in the UK are spending more than £1.3 billion a year on fast food. Almost a third of pocket money is thought to be spent on snacks eaten while travelling to and from school. This trend is compounded by the close proximity to schools of fast-food outlets. According to the Scottish Consumer Council (2001), school catering services face competition from local shops, cafes and takeaway establishments, which then forces schools to concentrate on the type of fast food popular with children, rather than on healthier alternatives. It is therefore not surprising to hear that 'Sales of snacks and confectionery continue to rise in the UK, outstripping those in all other European countries'. Nor is it surprising to hear that 'in 2000 around 675 million restaurant meals were eaten in the UK (an increase of almost 13% since 1995)'. Or that 'portion sizes are getting larger, particularly in "energy-dense" snacks and fast foods. "Supersizing" of fast foods is an increasingly popular trend in the UK' (CMO, 2002).

The American sociologist George Ritzer has argued that the fast-food industry is part of a much broader cultural and economic change which he terms 'McDonaldisation', which is characterised by an instrumental and efficiency-focused profit-maximising approach to the mass production and consumption of everything from food to high finance. *Rationalisation* processes include the tendency to *standardise* goods and services, including food, and the tendency to make things as *cost-effective, efficient and calculable* as possible. And, in order that what is produced is profitable, 'McDonaldisation' also seeks to control markets through extending outlet chains, and systematic advertising campaigns that sell a way of life just as much as the latest in burgers and shakes. The result is an economy and a society which become more like a conveyor belt, to produce and consume things as fast as possible, with less and less regard to their intrinsic value and whether or not they are good for you.

Using Ritzer's argument in terms of the fast-food industry, the aim is speed and standardisation of production and consumption, and the ability to produce and consume on a 24/7 basis. Food becomes a vehicle for profits to be made, rather than to satisfy appetites in the most nutritious way (if the latter occurs, it is a by-product, not the central objective). Because efficiency and profitability are the major concern, the focus is on how to standardise fast-food outlets, replicating them across the public sector in schools and hospital, railway stations and airport lounges.

However, as Ritzer goes on to argue, McDonaldisation is ultimately *irrational* for humanity. As he reflects, 'Rational systems are disenchanted; they have lost their magic and mystery and deny the human reason of the people who work within them or are served by them. In other words, rational systems are dehumanising' (Ritzer, 2001, p 23).

For example, fast food is *disenchanting*: people taste the double loading of sugar and salt on French fries, but not the potato; 'molly macbutter' and 'butter buds' have no butter (!); the turkey flavour in the frozen turkey dinner is artificial because the natural flavour has been removed in the processing; and whether you're in a hospital in Delhi or a shopping mall in Glasgow, one 'super-sized' high-carbohydrate meal is much the same as another. Fast food is also irrational because it may not be so cost-effective as was first assumed, if we take into account in particular the side effects of obesity associated with fast-food consumption, which costs the NHS millions of pounds every year. Continuing our theme of *irrationality*, one of the main food industry journals, *Eurofood* (2002b), aptly demonstrates the irrationality of our fast-food culture:

> A report carried out by the US National Alliance for Nutrition and Activity (NANA) looking into the cost to calorie ratio of foods from outlets such as fast-food chains, ice cream parlours, coffee shops and movie theatres, warns that super-sizing meals for a lot more food but only a little more money, could be contributing to the skyrocketing obesity rates. The report compared the price, calories and saturated fat in several fast foods. Its findings showed that the calories and saturated fat increased disproportionately to cost, which encouraged people to buy the bigger portions because they are better value. For example, upgrading from a Cinnabon Minibon to a Classic Cinnabon costs only 24% more, but delivers 123% more calories. The larger product also contains almost three-quarters of a day's worth of artery clogging saturated fat. (*Eurofood*, 2002b)

In summary, the social structural paradigm places the main focus on broader social influences in explaining the obesity trends described above. The structural emphasis, however, could be accused of treating individuals as victims unable to express constraint or choice over how much they engage with the fast-food culture. Nevertheless, the focus on lifestyle changes associated with post-industrialism and the impact of a fast-food industry on daily eating habits combine to provide powerful arguments that obesity is more of a social than a biological 'fact'. The medical paradigm does place some importance on the individual's engagement in lifestyle changes, whether in the form of dieting, as this chapter has emphasised, or by taking the appropriate exercise and engaging in more healthy eating choices. However, the latter are extensions of biomedical causes and remedies. Nevertheless, the medical and social structural paradigms should be viewed as complementary to each other in developing a multifaceted understanding, rather than as cancelling each other out. Indeed, this is the manner in which they are usually received; with the proviso mentioned earlier that one paradigm may be given more analytical and practical weighting than the other. Combined, the two paradigms view obesity as the complex, overlapping outcome of biology, social agency and social structure. One could say that biological and social structures generate mechanisms that provide the context within which social agents operate, constraining and enabling social agents in relation to lifestyle choices.

Taken together, they provide an understanding of how obesity emerges from the existence of real structures that are independent of human agency and interpretation, and which both constrain and present opportunities for social agents. Here, obesity is the result of actions taken and of patterns of behaviour adopted by social agents that are inherent parts of broader emergent powers, both biological and social. These powers cannot be observed directly (for example, we have still to locate an 'obese gene', or prove a causal link between fast-food markets and obesity), but they nevertheless produce biological and/or social mechanisms that we can observe (for example, differences in metabolic rate, food consumed and weight change; changes in work patterns/the rise of the fast-food industry). Moreover, it is through these mechanisms that social agents both give meaning to and act upon food consumption and body shape. Combining insights from both the medical and social paradigms resists reductive arguments, in the sense that the causes of obesity are not reduced to one process or event; rather, the biological, agential and social structural are moments or processes in a more holistic understanding of obesity.

However, some would challenge the very idea that obesity has a separate existence from how we socially construct it. The social constructionist paradigm argues that what exists (in this case, the obesity epidemic) depends on the meanings we give to obesity and that it is not an object outside how we socially construct it. According to this view, obesity is not a reality out there to be recorded objectively, but rather the outcome of how society constructs notions of 'normal' bodies and 'abnormal' bodies. In this view, both medical and social structural paradigms combine to strengthen the medicalisation of obesity.

Obesity as a social construction

For Berger and Luckmann (1991 [1967]), the social construction of reality means that people interact and enter reciprocal roles through which they create, foster and share meanings and concepts which they act upon and which form the basis of their social practice, to the point where those meanings and actions become inscribed in institutions and embedded in society as objective truths. Social constructionist perspectives differ in the extent to which they allow a reality outside of the meanings people actively share, with one end of the spectrum rejecting a separate reality and downplaying human agency and the other end subscribing to some belief in a reality beyond the social construction of reality, and so the relative independence of social agents (Burr, 2003). Nevertheless, social constructionists seek to challenge the very idea of an obesity epidemic. Before turning to a more detailed assessment of the social constructionist argument in relation to obesity and the body, we can obtain an understanding of why a social construction argument may be appropriate to obesity by reflecting on the validity of the definition of obesity – the BMI – as an accurate measure of obesity, and on the validity of research data supporting evidence of an obesity epidemic.

As explained earlier, the BMI scale is a measure of body mass. However, the scale does not distinguish between fat and muscle when defining obesity. In theory and in practice, a person classified as 'obese' may well be perfectly fit and have a normal range of fat. For example, an athlete may conceivably have a BMI of between 25 and 30 and yet be otherwise fit and healthy. The BMI also takes little account of age- and gender-related differences in the relationship between muscle and fat. When we get older, muscle usually turns to fat as part of the natural ageing process – defined in terms of the BMI scale, this process would register as a sign of obesity. Moreover, the link between weight increase and ill-health is perhaps more tenuous than we would like to think. As one study reminds us, we do not know whether two people with the same BMI but different amounts of fat have different risks for disease, because weight is only one factor related to disease (Garrow and Webster, 1985). One implication is that, while obesity may, for example, be the cause of premature death, death could just as easily be due to causes totally unrelated to a person's obesity. We do not know with any certainty, because the lines of causality are complex and operate across each other. For example, if someone has a pre-existing heart condition, he or she may be discouraged from taking exercise, resulting in weight gain. In such a case it would be strange to blame the weight gain for their demise. As Oliver (2006) suggests, the grounds for claiming that obesity is a major cause of death rather than one of a number of related possible contributing factors are extremely weak. Both Campos (2004) and Oliver (2006) argue that there is little by way of any statistically firm evidence that adiposity produces pathologies such as heart disease, diabetes, hypertension and deep-vein thrombosis, and so on, or that weight loss reduces our exposure to such health risks. Indeed, body fat can help to prevent disease, and moderately overweight people tend to live longer than people in the 'normal' weight range (Oliver, 2006, pp 2–5). Moreover, the risk of rising BMI and increased mortality is *exponential*, that is, increased mortality rises slowly until BMI reaches above 50%; before 50%, the connection is weak.

Of course, such criticism of the BMI scale and associated data does not lead to the conclusion that obesity is a moral panic without reality. Nevertheless, what the above critique perhaps does demonstrate is that definitions and data are difficult to pin down, are culture specific and have no simple connection to ill-health. According to the social constructionist paradigm this at least should serve to alert us to how obesity may be *socially constructed*.

Turning now to social construction, obesity and body politics, from a social constructionist perspective, obesity is linked to the body as a site of social control. As Turner (2008, p 149) puts it, 'obesity is not an empirical characteristic of unregulated bodies, but the effect of a language about bodies'. The body per se, as well as issues emerging from the body, such as weight and shape, provides a powerful means of governing what is normal, as opposed to abnormal, within populations (Turner, 2008). This can be more practically understood by reflecting for a moment on how we relate to and make sense of each other through a multitude of body-related symbols. We buy brand-named clothes and foods, sometimes because we think the quality is better than for non-branded, but for the most part because we are buying into a system of meanings about how we wish to be perceived by others in the social pecking order. In this respect, branded goods are purchased not only for their intrinsic value but also for what they symbolise for us and for others (Allen et al, 2007).

In the same manner, our dress sense, manner of expression, the roles we play out as mother, father, sister, brother, worker, manager, professional, and so on, are all symbols through which we relate to others. There is nothing natural or intrinsic about any of these symbols, they are all social constructions that give out social information about us and our place in the social world. Of course we change them and we challenge them, and often resist them as much as we embrace them, but nevertheless, they are inherent in social order and indeed in social control.

The point of the above is to stress that, as with roles and dress, so the body is a symbol, just as much as it is a natural entity. Our gestures and the way we make contact with others, as well as body shape, are all symbolic. The attraction for some of sporting icons is the images they provide of the ideal shape or what it means to be masculine or feminine. As Douglas notes, 'The social body constrains the way the physical body is perceived. The physical experience of the body ... sustains a particular view of society. There is a continual exchange of meaning between the two kinds of bodily experience so that each reinforces the other' (Douglas, 1970, p 93).

How does the above relate to a social constructionist understanding of obesity? The modern-day concern with obesity provides a powerful symbol of control over body size and shape, and, with it, over what is and is not an 'appropriate' lifestyle. In the modern world, where individuals are meant to be independent and self-seeking go-getters, responsible for their own health and welfare, and where notions of state dependency for anything from employment to social security handouts are frowned upon, then we can begin to understand from where the concern with obesity derives. In a symbolic sense, obesity stands in a state of deviancy in relation to current social aspirations about individual behaviour and moral obligations. Overweight is symbolic of decadence and an anti-entrepreneurial culture of dependency. The obese are a drain on public finances in an era of globalisation in which individuals are charged with responsibility for their own welfare (Townend, 2009, p 172). As Millman notes, 'Ours is a culture of personal responsibility; we are told to captain our own souls and "take responsibility" for our successes and failures' (Millman, 1980, p 155).

Becker (1997 [1963]) in particular drew attention to the way in which labelling – the process whereby socially defined identities are imposed or adopted – leads to the stigmatisation of an individual or group. Here, stigmatisation refers to the process whereby forms of social behaviour become the subject of social disapproval. In this respect, critiques of an unreflexive belief in obesity epidemics point to narratives of obesity promoted by health professionals and middle-class puritans and 'body' snobs who conjure up images of slothful working-class 'fatties' lacking willpower and self-respect. What Terry and Urla (1995, p 26) term 'embodied deviance ... the scientific and popular postulate that the bodies of subjects classified as deviant are essentially marked in some recognizable fashion.... Palpable and visible, the body's contours, anatomical features, processes, movements, and expressions are taken to be straightforward, accurate indications of an individual's essence and character'.

In this respect, obesity scaremongering is part and parcel of an irrational trend in society in which 'focusing upon one's diet and other lifestyle choices has become an alternative to prayer and righteous living in providing a means of making sense of life and death. "Healthiness" has replaced "Godliness" as a yardstick of accomplishment and proper living' (Lupton, 1995). Moreover, the present concern with obesity may perhaps also be part of a general concern about how people ought to live their lives and about what is deemed 'normal', 'acceptable' behaviour. Most crucially, it is about limiting risk, or more precisely, the fear of risk of becoming morally lax. Accordingly, those concerned with the 'plight of the obese' may appear to be liberal and caring about our health and well-being, but underneath this is a seething self-righteousness about how individuals ought and ought not to live their lives. For such people, it is argued, to be slothful and 'fat' in the modern era is the equivalent of living in sin.

In the above examples, the claim is that the lifestyles of particular groups are targeted as pathological. Engaging in smoking, drinking, creating the possibility of sexually transmitted diseases, eating fat, sugar and salt and avoiding too much exercise are associated more with 'the poor' and marginalised, the 'working classes', 'ethnic minorities'; in other words, 'deviant' groups. As Townend (2009, p 179) reflects, such 'moralising discourse reaches a peak on the issue of obesity, a condition which is both highly visible and directly associated with immorality in the sins of gluttony and sloth, and which is suffered disproportionately by people who are poor and/or working class'. Social constructionists recognise that the average weight of western populations may well be going up gradually. However, this may not be due to moral laxity but may have more to do with contemporary lifestyles, which tend to be more sedentary than the past. We now drive more, walk and exercise less; we tend to engage in relatively less manual work than in the past, and household appliances are easing labour-intensive domestic work. Some would argue that, measured against such social changes, it is perhaps to the credit of our common sense and self-restraint that we are not even heavier, on average, than we are (Lyons, 2003).

Conclusion

This chapter has argued that obesity can be understood as the complex interplay outlined by three paradigms: medical, social structural and social constructionist. Taken together, the medical and social structural illuminate the biological, agential and social structural moments or processes surrounding obesity. The two paradigms help us to theoretically position the multifaceted links between biology, agency and social structure as emergent relations. Combined, the two paradigms present powerful arguments against any simplistic re-reading of obesity as body politics. Measurements of obesity may differ and statistical data may only offer a rough idea of trends and causal directions, but these issues cannot spirit away obesity, which remains an issue of social importance and concern.

However, this chapter has also been at pains to explain the social constructionist argument that talk of an 'obesity epidemic' may be more mythology than reality. Social constructionists present a powerful case for viewing the mythology of obesity as a means of social control and a state of deviancy in relation to current social aspirations about individual behaviour and moral obligations.

Questions for further reflection

1 Explain the difficulties involved in defining someone as 'obese'.
2 To what extent is the constructionist approach compatible with taking a social structural approach to understanding obesity?
3 To what extent is the individual responsible for their weight?
4 Why is it argued by some that obesity is a political issue?

References

Allen, C.T., Fournier, S. and Miller, F. (2007) 'Brands and their meaning makers', in P. Curtis et al (eds), *Handbook of consumer psychology*, London: Psychology Press.

Becker, H.S. (1997 [1963]) *Outsiders: Studies in the sociology of deviance*, Glencoe: Free Press.

Berger and Luckmann (1991 [1967]) *The social construction of reality: A treatise in the sociology of knowledge*, London: Penguin

Brindal, E. et al (2008) 'Obesity and the effects of choice at a fast food restaurant', *Obesity Research & Clinical Practice*, vol 2, pp 111–17.

Burr, V. (2003) *An introduction to social constructionism*, London: Routledge.

Campos, P. F. (2004) *The obesity myth: Why America's obsession with weight is hazardous to your health*, New York: Gotham Books.

Carvel, J. (2002) 'Diet industry will be winner in battle of the bulge as Europe goes to fat', *Guardian*, 31 May.

CMO (Chief Medical Officer) (2002) *Annual report of the Chief Medical Officer*, London: Department of Health.

Commission of the European Communities (2005) *Promoting healthy diets and physical activity: A European dimension for the prevention of overweight, obesity and chronic diseases*, Green Paper, Brussels: European Commission .

Crossley, N. (2004) 'Fat is a sociological issue: obesity rates in late modern, "body-conscious" societies', *Social Theory & Health*, vol 2, no 3, pp 222–53.

DMCPRS (2003) *Data Monitor Consumer Product Market Research Study, Diet Watchers*, November.

Douglas, M. (1970) *Purity and danger: An analysis of concepts of pollution and taboo*, London: Routledge.

Eurofood (2002a) 'Breakfast habits on the change – Food Industry Report – UK', 7 November (http://findarticles.com/p/articles/mi_m0DQA/is_2002_Nov_7/ai_94448042/).

Eurofood (2002b) 'Super-sized meals and super-sized waists – Food Industry Report – fast food outlets criticized for portions and pricing', 4 July (http://findarticles.com/p/articles/mi_m0DQA/is_2002_July_4/ai_89077130/).

Food & Drink Weekly (2005) 'Study finds connection between fast food, obesity', 10 January.

Foresight (Government Office for Science) (2007) *Tackling obesities: Future choices*, Department of Innovation Universities and Skills (www.dius.gov.uk).

Garrow, J. (1996) 'Seven deadly sins', Saturday, 21–28 December, *British Medical Journal*, vol 313, no 7072, pp 1595–6.

Garrow, J.S. and Webster, J. (1985) 'Quetelet's index (W/H2) as a measure of fatness', *International Journal of Obesity*, vol 9, pp 147–53.

Halverson, R. (1993) 'Chains driving profits in fast-food lanes – fast-food restaurants in retail discount houses', *Discount Store News*, no 4, January.

Institute of Medicine (2004) *Childhood obesity in the United States: Fact and figures*, September (www.iom.edu/Object.File/Master/22/606/FINALfactsandfigures2.pdf).

International Obesity Taskforce (2009) (www.iotf.org/popout.asp?linkto=www.cdc.gov/nccdphp/dnpa/obesity/).

Johnson, A. (2008) 'Obesity', Speech by the Rt Hon Alan Johnson MP, Secretary of State for Health, 23 July (www.dh.gov.uk/en/News/Speeches/DH_087420).

Lichtman, S.W. et al (1992) 'Discrepancy between self-reported and actual caloric intake and exercise in obese subjects', *New England Journal Medicine*, vol 327, pp 1893–8.

Lupton, D. (1995) *The imperative of health: Public health and the regulated body*, London: Sage Publications.

Lyons, R. (2003) 'Weight watchers, review of Greg Critser's *Fat Land*', 25 June (www.spiked-online.com).

MacIntyre, A.M. (1998) 'Burden of illness review of obesity: are the true costs realised?', *Journal of the Royal Society for the Promotion of Health*, vol 118, no 76, pp 76–84.

Millman, M. (1980) *Such a pretty face: Being fat in America*, New York: Norton.

NCHS (National Centre for Health Surveys) (2008) 'Prevalence of overweight, obesity and extreme obesity among adults: United States, trends 1976–80 through 2005–2006' (www.cdc.gov/nchs/products/pubs/pubd/hestats/overweight/overweight_adult.pdf).

NEDAI (National Eating Disorders Association's Information) (2002) (www.NationalEatingDisorders.org).

New Statesman (2004) Leader, 'How to cut obesity', *New Statesman*, 31 May (www.newstatesman.com/200405310001).

NHANES (2006) 'Prevalence of overweight and obesity among adults: United States, 2003–2004', cited in International Obesity Taskforce, www.iotf.org/popout.asp?linkto=www.cdc.gov/nccdphp/dnpa/obesity/.

NHS (2009) *Annual Evidence Update. Childhood obesity: surveillance and prevention* (www.library.nhs.uk/PUBLICHEALTH/ViewResource.aspx?resID=311370&pgID=9).

Oliver, J. E. (2006) *Fat politics: The real story behind America's obesity epidemic*, Oxford: OUP.

Prentice, A.M. and Jebb, S. (1995) 'Obesity in Britain: gluttony or sloth?', *British Medical Journal* vol 311, pp 437–9 (12 August).

Ritzer, G. (2001) *Explorations in the sociology of consumption*, London: Sage.

Rosenheck, R. (2008) Obesity reviews, The International Association for the Study of Obesity, doi: 10.1111/j.1467–789X.2008.00477.

Ruppel Shell, E. (2003) *Fat wars. The inside story of the obesity industry*, London: Atlantic Books.

Sarlio-Lähteenkorva, S. (2001) 'Weight loss and quality of life among obese people', *Social Indicators Research*, vol 54, no 3, pp 329–54.

Schlosser, E. (2002) *Fast food nation: What the all-American meal is doing to the world*, London: Penguin.

Scottish Consumer Council (2001) 'National action needed for school meals in Scotland', November (http://scotcons.demonweb.co.uk/pressinfo/01news_re/nr11nati.pdf).

Scottish Health Survey (2003) 'Healthy weight' (www.scotland.gov.uk/Topics/Statistics/Browse/Health/TrendObesity).

Spencer, J. (2005) 'Implanted devices may fight obesity; tiny gadgets stimulate stomach, nervous system; awaiting trial results', *Wall Street Journal*, 9 August (www.technologypartners.com/press/Implanted_Devices.pdf).

Spitzack, C. (1987) 'Confession and signification: the systematic inscription of body consciousness', *Journal of Medicine and Philosophy*, vol 12, no 4, pp 357–69.

Terry, J. and Urla, J. (1995) *Deviant bodies: Critical perspectives on difference in science and popular culture*, Bloomington and Indianapolis: Indiana University Press.

Townend, L. (2009) 'The moralizing of obesity: A new name for an old sin?', *Critical Social Policy*, vol 29, no 2, pp 171–90.

Turner, S. (2008) *The body and society: Explorations in social theory* (3rd edn), London: Sage.

Walsh, J. (2001) 'Who ate all the burgers?', *Independent*, 13 July.

WHO (World Health Organization) (2005) *Obesity and overweight* (www.who.int/mediacentre/factsheets/fs311/en/index.html).

EIGHT

Conclusion

The intention of this book was to tackle the well-known and ongoing debate of medicalisation that is central to any literature in the field of the sociology of health and illness. The book also aimed to highlight the usefulness of social theory to a better understanding of contemporary social issues, including the rise of complementary and alternative health practices, the happiness industry, the MMR vaccine scare and the so-called 'epidemics' of binge drinking and obesity. From the academic experience of both authors, it was clear that although many students are very interested in these topics, they are also fearful both of social theory and of their ability to apply it confidently to areas of their own research. This book was therefore based upon a well-tried and tested course offered to students at the Glasgow Caledonian University that aimed to show, through the application of social theory to contemporary social issues, how theories can be usefully deployed to make better sense of health-related social issues that are often presented to us as uncontested or indisputable social facts.

It was also the intention of the book to highlight and illuminate the role that sociology itself plays in the creation of the discourse that surrounds the medicalisation thesis. This role, it was argued, is important to recognise because sociology as a body of knowledge is not separate from the object of its inspection and critical gaze, but also plays a crucial role in the construction and shaping of that object and, in this respect, the medicalisation thesis. In acknowledging this, it is hoped that this book will further the argument that the part that sociology plays in the medicalisation thesis in general, and in critiques of biomedicine in particular, needs to become far more transparent within the literature and ultimately to lend itself to a more fruitful debate for us all, one that can further strengthen and ultimately give more value to the wealth of intellectual ideas that already exist and are, in fact, drawn upon in the book.

With this in mind, the book has described key theories and concepts and examined how they shape our understanding of popular themes and issues within health, medicine and society. In particular, it has stressed how a range of concepts, including 'late modernity', 'modernity', 'risk society', 'moral panic', and so on, shape one's understanding of popular themes and issues such as the commodification of health and medicine, complementary and alternative medicine, the MMR debate, therapy and happiness, binge drinking and obesity, which are increasingly falling within the medical domain. The phrase 'shape one's understanding' is relevant here, as it signifies the creative process involved: concepts are active in *producing* different sources of knowledge that can just as often conflict as complement each other. An emphasis on the active role of concepts seems relevant, given that individuals in late modern society are now thought to be much more reflexive about a range of health and medical issues. Reflexivity implies not only that we are increasingly sceptical of the proclamations of health experts, but also that we are likely to be more sceptical of the truths espoused by sociologists concerning the role and nature of medicine in society. In writing the book, we have been keen to engage with a more reflexive audience that is less willing to accept one-sided critiques of medicine and reductive arguments concerning the causes of medicalisation.

In this respect, it is worth using these closing remarks to reflect on the underlying theme of the book, namely, to uncover medicalisation as a *process* defined by three interlinking encounters: the medical encounter, the social structural encounter and the encounter with the 'architecture of concepts and theories' that sociologists bring to the discussion. As the book has described through a series of examples, the medical encounter is defined by the expanding jurisdiction of medicine (institutionally, and as a pervasive language to reinterpret everyday social interactions) into non-medical domains. The social structural encounter refers to the dynamic structuring and restructuring of society, affecting the economy, culture and politics, which we label variously as 'moral panics', 'risk-conscious society', 'modernity' and 'late modernity', and so on. These social structures exert their own impact on medicalisation; they can facilitate it, transform how and when it occurs and so influence whether we view it negatively or positively; they can help to determine what the prospects for demedicalisation are and, indeed, what forces are advancing the medicalisation of society. Overlapping this is the conceptual encounter. As well as signifying structural changes, patterns and events, 'late modernity' and 'moral panic', and so on, are also *conceptual products, modes of understandings*, all of which are understood differently by social theorists, who socially construct ways of knowing and ways of acting towards 'medicalisation'.

For example, we noted how different readings of the political economy of medicine in modern industrial society produced different ways of knowing medicalisation. Illich's powerful and insightful critique of the negative consequences of medicine in society accords very well with aspects of the evidence presented with respect to systemic medical error, misapplication of drugs and the close influence of the pharmaceutics industry in representing medicalisation as both negative and omnipotent. The fact that Illich chooses not to give adequate recognition to the positive contributions medicine has made to the fight against disease and the promotion of population-wide health is his way of consolidating this reading of medicalisation. However, as we also noted, from the standpoint of the Marxist approach to medicine, as mediated by class struggle and commodification, medicine is presented as contradictory in its effects on individuals and on society as a whole, with medicalisation holding costs and benefits for both the capitalist class and the proletariat. According to the Marxist approach, medical practice and its consequences are mediated by definitions of health and illness which are inscribed within the capitalist economy and the requirements for functionally productive labour, as well as by the requirement that use values and social needs, such as those for healthcare, either enhance or, at worst, do not set insurmountable limits to the requirements of the capitalist economy for profit. Illich's conceptual encounter produces a different reading of modernity to that of Marxist conceptual encounters, and therefore a different way of knowing medicalisation in terms of the nature and scope of the expanding jurisdiction of medicine in society.

We found a similar dynamic at work when we discussed the relationship between orthodox and alternative medicine. The emphasis placed by Giddens on the reflexive potentials inherent in late modernity seems to offer scope for articulating this relationship as more of a challenge to orthodox medicine's authority in terms of the wider societal erosion of traditional economic, cultural and political structures and the opening up of new structures that agents negotiate more critically and reflexively. However, Habermas and Weber provide a different reading of late modernity, which then produces a different way of understanding the relationship between orthodox and alternative medicines. The tension between 'life' and 'system' worlds, to which Habermas draws our attention, combined with Weber's approach to professional power, suggests that it would be wrong to see this challenge as one simply based on the rejection of orthodox medicine for CAM. Instead, the relationship is represented in ways that allow for the possibility of a struggle to integrate the best aspects of CAM with those of biomedicine and, by so doing, saving biomedicine from an uncoupled systems world by recoupling it with the values and practices associated with the life world. This latter reading of late modernity can conceptualise the state vis-à-vis orthodox and alternative medicine as being in tension between *incorporation* and *integration*. When *system* imperatives of cost cutting, efficiency and administration are uppermost, then the state leans towards attempting to impose abstract managerial discourses across CAMs that take less account of the particularities of their individual practices and skill sets and more account of the need to shadow the administrative fiat of orthodoxy. However, when 'life world' imperatives gain a voice, this can be seen in the extent to which the state is genuinely searching for professional codes of conduct and training that are sensitive to the specifics of the alternative medicine they are designed to regulate and recognises the underpinning philosophy that comes with alternative medicine, rather than expunging its holistic philosophy for a reworked Cartesian dualism. Again, what emerges from the dispute over the nature of late modernity is an awareness that different conceptual encounters with it (in this case Giddens and Habermas) produce different ways of knowing the relationship between orthodox and alternative medicine and what they imply for medicalisation in terms of the nature and scope of the expanding jurisdiction of medicine in society.

We also saw these encounters at work in respect of the self-help and happiness industry. Salerno, Furedi and Giddens all draw attention to the cultural turn towards therapy, but each has different readings that then have ramifications for how they see therapy culture in relation to medicalisation. Salerno explains therapy culture as the product of charlatans creating a market out of people's fears, which have their origin in the move away from the securities of place and identity offered by traditional society. Salerno makes a distinction between medicine proper, which has a distinct knowledge base and professional group legitimised to know and act on the body, and outsiders who are not authorised to practise and who represent a form of disempowerment by offering individuals quick-fix, medically based solutions to social and personal problems. For Salerno, medicine is separate from medicalisation. For Furedi, therapy culture represents the evolving power of medicine in society. Medicalisation, for Furedi, spreads out from traditional medical institutions to develop its powers of circulation within the capillaries of society. In this sense, while Habermas's approach to late modernity revealed the broadening of medicalisation across orthodox and alternative medicines, and the state as the legitimating agency with powers to integrate alternative medicine, Furedi places emphasis on the ways in which this broadening takes on a new dimension, as part of the everyday language of society, which he terms therapy culture. In both cases, medicalisation is represented as a negative force in society. Giddens, on the other hand, sees in therapy culture the potential benefits of medicine and of demedicalisation, when he argues that individuals have the capacity to be critical and reflective and so are well able to make their own up minds about what they get out of the self-help movement. And indeed, not all individuals choose to get involved, which implies that a certain level of healthy scepticism and pragmatism pervades individual choices when it comes to people's relationship with the self-help and happiness industry. In other words, Giddens reconceptualises relations of late modernity and medicine in terms of scepticism and resistance to its assumed omnipotent medicalising pretensions.

As this book has also noted, Beck's concept of 'risk society' is yet another way of encountering medicine and medicalisation. Beck's thesis suggests that, on the one hand, science remains a pivotal source of knowledge about the world, while on the other hand it is also the subject of continual scrutiny and scepticism regarding its claims. We seek the assistance and authority of science, while at the same time we appear to question the validity of its claims and worry over the objectivity of its findings, sometimes to the point where we are unsure about what to believe for the best in areas affecting our well-being. We examined the merits of the concept of risk society for an understanding of the contradictory location of medical science in modern society, with particular reference to the MMR controversy. The chapter represents medicalisation in terms of this contradictory location; arguing that the extent to which risk society offers a challenge to the onward march of medicalisation is debatable. In one respect, the attention paid to reflexive individuals and parents challenging the authority of medicine over MMR and its links to autism suggests that this may be the case. However, closer inspection reveals not so much a challenge as insecurity and collective stasis about alternatives. The fall in the number of MMR vaccinations is not met by any wider resistance to medicine itself; it is more a matter of parents voting with their feet and hoping that this will generate more awareness within medicine itself concerning MMR. It could just as easily be argued that being exposed to a variety of potential risks and being more reflexive of such information makes individuals more vulnerable, not necessarily more empowered to check the onward march of medicalisation.

The concept of moral panic was another way of representing the dynamics involved in the medicalisation of society. The example of binge-drinking youth was developed to explain how moral panics promote the medicalisation of society by converting social structural maladies into seemingly more manageable and resolvable personal failings and medically related matters underpinning binge drinking. We drew on evidence from the media, health professionals and government sources to explain how each of these sources treats binge drinking as something objective, to be either cured or controlled. While the real negative consequences of alcohol excess are never in doubt, the chapter also argued that social problems are never neutrally observed, nor do they exist as objects of investigation. Social issues and problems are also the source of social construction, and these constructions tend to express social anxieties, fears and insecurities that may also echo broader structural changes and help to construct our understandings of what is driving medicalisation.

Obesity too was understood in terms of the complex interplay outlined by three paradigms: medical, social structural and social constructionist, all of which have implications for the ways in which medicalisation is represented. The medical and social structural paradigms illuminate the biological, agential and social structural moments or processes surrounding obesity. The two paradigms help us to theoretically position the multifaceted links between biology, agency and social structure as emergent relations. The paradigms also act as the dividing line between medicine and medicalisation. As noted in the chapter discussing obesity, medicalisation is defined by the way in which medicine marginalises, without ignoring, the social structural paradigm and places emphasis on the body and lifestyle/dietary choices made by individuals, which can then be treated through medical intervention and dietary regimes. Nevertheless, in accepting the social reality of obesity measures and statistical trends, the social structural paradigm may inadvertently implicate itself in the medicalisation of obesity. However, the chapter was also at pains to explain the social constructionist paradigm and its argument that talk of an 'obesity epidemic' may be more mythology than reality. Social constructionists present a powerful case for viewing the mythology of obesity as a means of social control and a state of deviancy in relation to current social aspirations concerning proper and improper individual behaviour and moral obligations. Seen through the social constructionist lens, medicalisation is represented as part of medicine's extension into the field of body politics and surveillance over society.

It is in the above ways that the book has sought to engage with a more reflexive audience, less willing to accept one-sided critiques of medicine and reductive arguments concerning the causes of medicalisation.

Further reading

Asthana, A. (2003) 'Row over new "link" between MMR jab and autism', *Guardian*, 2 November.

Austin, B.S. (1999) 'Fat, loathing and public health: the complicity of science in a culture of disordered eating, *Culture, Medicine and Psychiatry*, vol 23, pp 245–68.

Barthes, D.J.P. (1998) *Epidemiology in medical practice*, London: Pearson.

Barton, P. et al (1997) *Child protection. Risk and the moral order*, London: Macmillan Press Ltd.

BBC News (2004) 'Fat profits making dough', 17 March (www.news.bbc.co.uk).

Beaglehole, R. et al (1993) *Basic epidemiology*, Geneva: World Health Organisation.

Beck, U. et al (1994) *Reflexive modernity*, Cambridge: Polity Press.

Bordo, S. (1995) 'Beyond overeating', *New England Journal of Medicine*, vol 332, no 10, pp 673–4.

British Medical Association (2003) *Adolescent health*, British Medical Association Report.

British Medical Journal (1995) 'Education and debate: obesity in Britain: gluttony or sloth?', vol 311, pp 437–9.

Bunton, R. and Burrows, R. (1995) 'Consumption and health in the "epidemiological" clinic of late modernity', in R. Bunton et al (eds), *The sociology of health promotion*, London: Routledge.

Cant, S. and Sharma, U. (1996) 'The professionalisation of complementary medicine in the UK', *Complementary Therapies in Medicine*, vol 4, pp 157–62.

Cant, S. and Sharma, U. (1996) 'The reluctant profession – homoeopathy and the search for legitimacy', *Work, Employment and Society*, vol 9, pp 743–62.

Carvel, J. and O'Hara, M. (2009) 'Binge drinking Britain: surge in women consuming harmful amounts of alcohol', Guardian Online (www.guardian.co.uk/society/2009/may/06/binge-drinking-women).

Christie, J., Fischer, D., Kozup, J.C., Smith, S., Burton, S. and Creyer, E.H. (2001): 'The effects of bar-sponsored alcohol beverage promotions across binge and non-binge drinkers', *Journal of Public Policy and Marketing*, vol 20, no 2, pp 240–53.

Daily Mail Online (2002) 'Binge drinking increases breast cancer risk', 22 March (www.dailymail.co.uk/health/article-106324/Binge-drinking-increases-breast-cancer-risk.html).

Daily Mail Online (2004) 'Blair: Binge drinking is new British disease', 20 May (www.dailymail.co.uk/news/article-303621/Blair-Binge-drinking-new-British-disease.html).

Department of Health (1995) *Sensible drinking: The report of an inter-departmental working group*, London: Department of Health.

Department of Health (2009) 'There were 602 cases of measles reported in England and Wales by the end of April 2009. This is double the number confirmed for the same period last year' (www.dh.gov.uk/en/Publicationsandstatistics/Bulletins/theweek/DH_100622).

Dew, K. (1999) 'Epidemics, panics and power: representations of measles and mumps vaccines', *Health*, vol 3, no 4, p 379.

ECO (2005) 14th European Congress on Obesity, International Obesity Task Force Press Release, June (www.iotf.org/media/iotfmetsynjun1.pdf).

Ernst, E. (2009) 'Harmless homeopathy?', *International Journal of Clinical Rheumatology*, vol 4, no 1, pp 7–10.

Featherstone, C. and Forsyth, L. (1997) *Medical marriage: The new partnership between orthodox and complementary medicine*, Forres: Findhorn Press.

Fenton, S. and Charsley, K. (2000) 'Epidemiology and sociology as incommensurate games: accounts from the study of health and ethnicity', *Health*, vol 4, no 4, pp 403–25.

Fisher, B.L. and Schauer, P. (2002) 'Medical and surgical options in the treatment of severe obesity', *American Journal of Surgery*, vol 184, no 6B, pp 1274–5.

Fisher, P. and Ward, A. (1994) 'Complementary medicine in Europe', *British Medical Journal*, vol 309, no 9, pp 107–11.

Freund, P.E. and McGuire, M. (2003) *Health, illness and the social body: A critical sociology*, London: Pearson.

Furnham, A. and Kirkaldy, B. (1996) 'The health beliefs and behaviours of clients of orthodox and complementary medicine', *British Journal of Clinical Psychology*, vol 35, pp 49–61.

Giddens, A. (1990) *The consequences of modernity*, Cambridge: Polity Press.

Government White Paper (2003) *Respect and responsibility – taking a stand against anti-social behaviour*, White Paper.

Grant, M. and Litvak, J. (1998) *Drinking patterns and their consequences*, Washington, DC: ICAP.

Guardian (2000) '55 cancer patients get wrong test results', 17 June.

Guldberg, H. (2005) 'MMR, autism and politics' (www.spiked-online.com/Articles/0000000CA59F.htm).

Harrison, S. and Ahamad, W.U. (2002) 'Medical autonomy and the UK state 1975 to 2025', in S. Nettleton and U. Gustafsson (eds) *The sociology of health and illness reader*, Cambridge: Polity.

Heather, N. (1995): 'Interpreting the evidence on brief interventions for excessive drinkers: the need for caution', *Addiction*, vol 30, pp 287–96.

Hobson-West, P. (2003) 'Understanding vaccination resistance: moving beyond risk, *Health, Risk & Society*, vol 5, no 3, pp 273–83.

Institute of Alcohol Studies (2003) *Factsheet: Young people and alcohol*, Cambridge: Institute of Alcohol Studies.

International Centre for Alcohol Policies (1997) *The limits of binge drinking*, Report 2, April (www.icap.org/publications/report2.html).

Jernigan, D.H. (2001) *Global status report: Alcohol and young people*, Geneva: WHO.

Kendell, R.E., de Roumanie, M. and Ritson, E.B. (1983): 'Effect of economic changes on Scottish drinking habits 1978–1982', *British Journal of Addiction*, vol 78, no 4, pp 365–79.

Leontaridi, R. (2003) *Alcohol misuse: How much does it cost?*, London: Cabinet Office.

Lowenberg, J. and Davis, F. (1994) 'Beyond medicalisation–demedicalisation: the case of holistic health', *Sociology of Health and Illness*, vol 16, pp 579–99.

Lupton, D. (2003) 'Theoretical perspectives on medicine and society', in D. Lupton, *Medicine and culture*, London: Sage.

Marsh, P. (2001) 'In praise of bad habits. The dangers of "healthism" – and the good thing about risk', 22 November (www.spiked-online.com).

McCormick, B., Stone, I. and Corporate Analytical Team (2007) 'Economic costs of obesity and government intervention', *Obesity Reviews*, vol 8, supplement 1, pp 161–4.

Mizen, P. (2004) *The changing state of youth*, London: Palgrave.

MORI (2000) *Alcohol and society: Research study conducted by MORI for the Portman Group*, Home Office Research Study No 108, London: HMSO.

Mulhall, A. (1996) *Epidemiology, nursing and health: New perspectives*, London: Macmillan.

National Audit Office (2001) *Handling clinical negligence claims in England*, London: National Audit Office.

Norström, T. (ed) (2002) *Alcohol in postwar Europe: Consumption, drinking patterns, consequences and policy responses in 15 European countries*, Stockholm: Almqvist & Wiksell International.

Observer (2002) 'I'm simply bemused by the science and not fully persuaded either way', 10 February.

Pietroni, P. (1992) 'Beyond the boundaries: the relationship between general practice and complementary medicine', *British Medical Journal*, vol 305, pp 564–6.

Rennie, K.L. and Jebb, S.A. (2005) 'Prevalence of obesity in Great Britain', *Obesity Reviews*, vol 6, no 1, pp 11–12.

Rimm, E., Williams, P., Fosher, K., Criqui, M. and Stampfer, M.J. (1999) 'Moderate alcohol intake and lower risk of coronary heart disease', *British Medical Journal*, vol 319, pp 1523–8.

Saks, M. (1992) 'The paradox of incorporation: acupuncture and the medical profession in modern Britain', in M. Saks (ed) *Alternative medicine in Britain*, Oxford: Clarendon Press.

Saks, M. (1995) 'The role of professions: power, interest and causality', in M. Saks, *Professions and the public interest*, London: Routledge.

Saks, M. (2003) *Orthodox and alternative medicine: Politics, professionalisation and health care*, London: Sage.

Sobal, J. and Stunkard, A.J. (1989) 'Socioeconomic status and obesity: a review of the literature', *Psychological Bulletin*, vol 105, no 2, pp 260–75.

Stunkard, A.J. and Sorensen, T.I.A. (1993) 'Obesity and socioeconomic status – a complex relation', *New England Journal of Medicine*, vol 329, pp 1036–7.

Stuttaford, A. (2004) 'The fat police – food fight: The inside story of the food industry, America's obesity crisis, and what we can do about it', *National Review Online*, January (www.nationalreview.com).

Szasz, T. (1961) 'The uses of naming and the origin of the myth of mental illness', *American Psychology*, vol 16, pp 59–65.

USDMO (2005) 'The US diet market outlook to 2008: future profit opportunities for low carb and other fast growth diets', *Business Insights*, 1 February.

Vincent, C. (2001) 'Adverse events in British hospitals: Preliminary retrospective record review', *British Medical Journal*, vol 332, no 7285, pp 517-19.

Waitzkin, H. (2000) *The second sickness: Contradictions of capitalist health care,* Lanham, MD: Rowman and Littlefield.

Walker, L.A. and Budd, S. (2002) 'UK the current state of regulation of complementary and alternative medicine', *Complementary Therapies in Medicine*, vol 10, pp 8–13.

White, I., Altmann, D. and Nanchahal, K. (2000) *'Optimal' levels of alcohol consumption for men and women at different ages, and the all-cause mortality attributable to drinking*, London: London School of Hygiene and Tropical Medicine.

WHO (2008) Congress on Traditional Medicine, Speech by Dr Margaret Chan, Director-General of the World Health Organisation (www.who.int/dg/speeches/2008/20081107/en/index.html).

Wilkins, M.R. and Kendall, M.J. (1985) 'Discourse on excess and binge drinking a side line of the positive role of moderate drinking on health', *British Medical Journal*, vol 291, p 134.

Williams, J. (2004) 'Facts that should change the world', *New Statesman*, 17 May.

Index

DATE DUE

ILL#69860262	WAU 11-7-10
GAYLORD	PRINTED IN U.S.A.